Reading Dee-Dee's piece of work w invigorating experience I have had wit in sometime. Through her wisdom s of harm reduction and the 12 steps and shown the unique transparencies they each share. Dee-Dee has created a masterful book which will surely become required reading in colleges and schools with alcohol and drug counselor education programs. Thanks, Dee-Dee, for bringing us back to our roots while hopefully propelling us further forward.

---Warren A. Daniels, III, BA, CADC-II, ICADC, CCJP; Executive Director, Community Recovery Resources; Chairman, California Foundation for the Advancement of Addiction Professionals; Past President, the California Association of Alcohol and Drug Abuse Counselors (CAADAC).

This book is a fabulous collection of voices representing transformative experiences into the paradigm of harm reduction. The stories draw you into the personal worlds of professionals and clients, and how they construct pathways for feeling, thinking, and acting on solutions to addictions. Read how some struggled through medical/disease-oriented models that ended up constraining them and their client's progress to health. And read how they came to think there was another way to approach — harm reduction.

---Jane Peller, LCSW; Professor, Northeastern University, Chicago; co-author, *Recreating Brief Therapy.*

This book is a must read for students of addiction treatment. Dee-Dee Stout passionately chronicles the evolution of harm reduction in the U.S. by sharing stories she collected of how leaders of the harm reduction movement - with and without 12-Step experience - came to their current practice of substance abuse treatment. As the field of addiction treatment continues to evolve, it behooves all of us to read this thoughtful, provocative book that tells the principals of harm reduction and demonstrates how its roots lie in the history of Alcoholics Anonymous.

---Cathy McDonald, MD, MPH; Medical Consultant, Thunder Road Teen Drug Treatment Program and Tobacco Treatment Specialist; Oakland, CA.

This book powerfully documents the history of the harm reduction movement through compelling personal narratives from some of the most well-known harm reductionists in the country. From her unique perspective as a self-proclaimed "12-Stepper" who came to harm reduction "kicking and screaming," Dee-Dee Stout weaves together stories that bridge the worlds of 12-Step and harm reduction, long held to be enemies. This critical selection of stories reveals the many different paths these people have taken to harm reduction, and opens our hearts to the importance of treating all drug users with compassion and humanity, no matter what we call ourselves. This book should be read by anyone interested in helping people with drug problems in America.

---Juliana van Olphen, Ph.D., M.P.H., Assistant Professor, Department of Health Education, College of Health and Human Services, San Francisco State University, San Francisco, California.

COMING TO HARM REDUCTION KICKING & SCREAMING

Looking for Harm Reduction in a 12-Step World

Dee-Dee Stout

AuthorHouse™
1663 Liberty Drive
Bloomington, IN 47403
www.authorhouse.com
Phone: 1-800-839-8640

©*2009 Dee-Dee Stout. All rights reserved.*

No part of this book may be reproduced, stored in a retrieval system, or transmitted by any means without the written permission of the author.

First published by AuthorHouse 9/4/2009

ISBN: 978-1-4389-9547-2 (sc)

Library of Congress Control Number: 2009906480

Printed in the United States of America
Bloomington, Indiana

This book is printed on acid-free paper.

In memory of Mike

Table of Contents

Foreword	ix
Introduction	xiii
Suggestions for using this book and Acknowledgements	xvii
Preface	xxi
What is this thing called Harm Reduction?	1
Will the real AA please stand up?	12
The Oldtimers	**23**
Dan Bigg	23
Patt Denning	30
Tom Horvath	39
Marc Kern	44
Jeannie Little	49
G. Alan Marlatt	56
William (Bill) Miller	62
Lisa Moore	69
Stanton Peele	75
Fred Rotgers	80
Andrew Tatarsky	87
The 12-Stepping Harm Reductionists	**95**
Allan Clear	95
Annie Fahy	99
Mark Kinzly	105
Lochlan McHale	109
Steve M.	115
Edward Reed	119
Chuck Ries	122
Pam Smithstan	131

Dee-Dee Stout	137
Tommie (Larry) Walton	147
Imani Woods	153

In conclusion	156
A few resources	159
Appendices	162
Endnotes	166
Index	170

FOREWORD

Dee-Dee Stout is to be congratulated for providing readers with basic information about harm reduction in the field of addiction treatment and policy. When it comes to traditional treatment for people who are experiencing problems with their use of alcohol and/or other drugs, the situation is similar to approaching a traffic light at an intersection on Substance Use Road. For the driver/user, the light is either RED (stop using and maintain your abstinence) or GREEN (keep using on the "high" way). As pointed out in this book, the stop sign has a built-in message: your next step on your journey should be to attend a 12-Step program with all the other alcoholic drunk drivers and admit your powerlessness when it comes to the disease, and to turn your navigational control system over to a "Higher Power." No wonder so many users run the red light and continue down the path of their ongoing use, looking for the next green light.

When it comes to harm reduction, the traffic light is YELLOW at the intersection. Here the message is in the middle, above the green light and below the red. This middle-way light signals the driver to slow down and to be aware of the cross traffic and the potential harm that could occur if one continues to drive mindlessly ahead, as if the light were turning green instead of red. A related marker is the YIELD sign, often presented in the form of a yellow triangle. By yielding instead of driving on and ignoring this road sign, the driver has the opportunity to wait and see before proceeding ahead at the same pace.

For drivers who are unwilling or unable to stop and maintain abstinence at the red light (a high threshold requirement), harm reduction offers a low-threshold alternative, an opportunity to take stock and evaluate the consequences of one's driving experiences on the road of life, including positive trips (the thrill of getting high or the relief that drugs provide for tension-reduction or "numbing out" of negative emotional states) and bad trips (getting arrested for a DUI or causing damage to oneself, fellow passengers, or other drivers and pedestrians). This stocktaking is a key element of harm reduction: weighing the pros and cons of one's behavior and moving toward making a decision to be a safer driver. Harm reduction therapy provides users with a course of action that is similar to a safe-driving program: the driver is taught safe driving skills, including being mindful of traffic patterns and the behaviors of other drivers, enhancing awareness of speed limits and other rules of the road. Problem behaviors such as tail-gating (following another user's vehicle too closely) and speeding (including being high on speed behind the wheel) are addressed.

When it comes to drug policy, harm reduction provides new avenues for success for working with people with drug problems. Instead of the War on Drugs and the policy of Zero Tolerance, harm reduction fosters programs that can help prevent or treat individuals who have developed problems. It truly is a 'user friendly' approach, one that encourages users to seek treatment instead of being incarcerated (as is the case in the Drug Court programs) and to work with other users in a collaborative, helpful manner (as is the case in most needle-exchange programs for injecting drug users). Other programs that provide housing for homeless alcoholics who are allowed to drink in their apartments may save both lives and money (such a "Housing First" program in Seattle saved taxpayers over $4 million a year in reduced medical costs). Public policy support for medical marijuana programs is also consistent with harm reduction principles. With the new political administration now running the government in the nation's capital, there is hope that things will move away from the moral model of addiction (addicts have no will power and deserve to be locked up for their sins) and embrace a more holistic and empathic approach designed to provide help and assistance for our citizens who are experiencing harmful consequences associated with their substance use.

I would like to conclude with a strong vote of gratitude for the contributions that Dee-Dee Stout has brought to the field of addiction treatment and public policy. Her stories of people involved in the field, including those who were initially strongly opposed to any harm reduction programs, will have a major impact on treatment providers, politicians, policy makers and, most of all, active users. This book provides a strong shining YELLOW light for all drivers on the road of drug use. Thanks, Dee-Dee, for your very helpful roadmap for recovery.

G. Alan Marlatt, Ph.D.
University of Washington
Seattle, WA

INTRODUCTION

- ***Harm Reduction****: a word that has inspired a range of responses from hope to hysteria.*
- ***Harm Reduction****: a word that has been defined over and over again, yet still causes confusion.*
- ***Harm Reduction****: a journey taken by many who were determined to change the way we look at drug users.*

This book looks at harm reduction from the perspective of the people who have been working for years to spread this new paradigm to advocacy for a reformed drug policy, to the criminal justice system, to drug treatment and to public health. It is a unique way of crafting history, asking the people involved to tell their stories as they lived them. The stories come from two general groups: those who were "born harm reductionists" in that they didn't struggle much to embrace the values embodied in this humane and pragmatic approach and those who, generally because of their own personal involvement in recovering from substance misuse, had to wrestle with significant conflicts in order to come to harm reduction. This latter group represents the "kicking and screaming" people who, like the author, spent years developing the strength to change some of their deepest held beliefs about the nature of drug abuse, treatment, recovery and drug policy.

While the United States has been pursuing a world wide disastrous "War on Drugs," at home we have strict prohibition against certain intoxicating substances but not others, and our prisons have become warehouses for people convicted of little else than using illegal drugs. Our "zero tolerance" policies deprive poor people of their housing, children of their education, many people of their jobs and all of us of basic right to privacy. Our bodies no longer belong to us. We have been stripped of the right to govern what we put into our bodies; moreover the government can test our blood and urine and judge that we are criminals.

Despite this overwhelming governmental presence, perhaps as big an obstacle to the harm reduction movement - and to the "kicking and screaming" contributors in this book - has been the monolithic and unshakeable belief in the 12-Steps of Alcoholics Anonymous as the only viable treatment model. The beliefs, teachings and offshoot treatment methods in the United States have largely been derived from the customs (not to be confused with the 12-Traditions) of the 12-Step model. Despite not being a treatment method, this model has become, in fact, the main component of substance abuse treatment in 93% of all programs in the United States, even though its own co-founder, Bill Wilson, counseled otherwise. It has also become enmeshed in the "zero tolerance" criminal justice system, with AA and NA meeting secretaries signing attendance cards mandated by the courts, and treatment programs ignoring the basic principle of confidentiality by reporting back to those same judges and courts.

The 12-Step phenomena has also found its way into the cultural beliefs and attitudes of the typical American, who now believes that "addiction" is always a disease and only by continuous, lifetime attendance at 12-Step meetings and complete abstinence can a person hope to stop an inevitable decline to death. That no one can recover from this disease. That it takes life-long vigilance and attendance to remain "in recovery." And, finally, that people with this disease are different from the rest of the human race and that no one but others with the disease can fully understand or be of much use in treating it.

Given this potent combination of political, legal and cultural restrictions, it is no wonder that many otherwise sane and humane people, including 12-Steppers, have fallen prey to the disease and criminal models. The stories in this book give the reader an intimate look into the feelings, values and conflicts of people who have been leaders, followers and converts to harm reduction.

Coming to Harm Reduction Kicking & Screaming

Sometimes the most challenging thing about harm reduction is to recognize and adopt what, on the surface, may seem like common sense principles if one substituted the word "food" for the word "drugs." There are many lists of harm reduction principles. These are some of the basic ones:

- *First, do no harm! Jail, loss of job, etc. is more harmful than drug use.*
- *People have always used drugs.*
- *People can, and do, make rational decisions despite drug use.*
- *People have sovereignty over what they put into their bodies.*
- *Punishing people for using drugs creates lying, crime and shame.*
- *Not all drug use is abuse.*
- *Drug abuse is a health, not a legal, concern.*
- *Treatment must take into account individual differences.*
- *Change is slow, with many setbacks.*
- *People who have caused harm to others can rejoin their communities.*

The author, through her selection of stories, helps the reader see that the 12-Step fellowship did not start out to be the one and only truth about alcoholism (addiction), but rather a suggestion for a path taken by Dr. Bob and Bill Wilson that they felt might help others. The development of new slogans, customs, rules and beliefs that one identifies with 12-Step meetings and practice, does not necessarily reflect the intention of these two men (e.g. "take the cotton out of your ears and put it in your mouth" or the practice of having to identify as a "newcomer" if one has a slip, etc.). Perhaps this book will help retrieve the 12-Step tradition from the treatment world, allowing it to take its place as a spiritual fellowship, and allow those offering treatment to pay full attention to what the evidence points to as effective, freed from decades of mistaken beliefs.

Dee-Dee Stout

    This book chronicles the journeys that many people have taken, and it is my hope that it will create a new path for the reader. These personal stories often peer behind the curtain of long held biases, exposing the "wizard" (drug abuse) as a human phenomenon rather than an all-powerful magical force.   I hope you enjoy these readings as much as I did.

Patt Denning, Ph.D.
Harm Reduction Therapy Center
San Francisco, CA

SUGGESTIONS FOR USING THIS BOOK AND ACKNOWLEDGEMENTS

If you're reading this book, *THANK YOU*!! Much work and many long hours have gone into this little guide to harm reduction and 12-Step. I'd like to suggest, somewhat boldly, that this is not an ordinary book – you know, the kind you must start reading from the beginning and then read all the way through for it to make some sense. In fact, I'll suggest that, instead, you read only the parts that you think you'll find interesting – perhaps sections that might offer you a new perspective on harm reduction, or the story of someone you've always wanted to know more about. It is unimportant how you read it; what is more important is that you read it (with my apologies for any implied arrogance).

Writing this book, I was fortunate to have access to some of the most influential and well-known people in the field of harm reduction, whose stories are mostly found in the section called "Oldtimers." They provide fascinating reading from people who never saw why the rest of the United States believed so strongly in the medical, or disease, model and abstinence. Begin here if your interest is more in learning about how some people did *not* come to abstinence-only in their work in addictions, how they see harm reduction and what brought them to these concepts and principles. While discussing the "Oldtimers," I do want to acknowledge one important "Oldtimer" whose story could not be among these except here in passing: Edith Springer from New York City. Unfortunately, Edith was unable to be a direct part of this project though I am told she would be fully supportive of this book. The field of harm reduction and this book certainly wouldn't be possible without her considerable contributions to our field. Thank you, Edith!

In another section of the book, I was honored to have more stories than I could print! These are the stories of those who are or were 12-Steppers[1] and somehow found ourselves coming to harm reduction - sometimes kicking and screaming - but *coming* nonetheless! The stories that I could not use here were ones from students, needle exchange program consumers, former clients, colleagues, and others (the book would have been far too long). I hope someday to share these stories as they warmed my heart and convinced me even more of the value of such biographies to shift the culture of alcohol and other drugs treatment from one of dividedness to one of openness to harm reduction and all perspectives.

Another chapter in *Kicking and Screaming* that was incredibly enjoyable to work on and which brought me many surprises was "Will the Real AA please stand up?" Here, you'll find a chapter packed with both interesting tidbits and detailed historical notes of the harm reduction in the original Alcoholics Anonymous (AA). I was especially thrilled that Ernie Kurtz, the eminent AA historian and academic, agreed to review this chapter. I thank him for providing valuable suggestions that added clarity, interest, and generally improved the content of the chapter. This is the most technical of the chapters, and I hope you will take the time to look through it. I found many unusual accounts of AA history while researching this chapter and hope that some of the myths of AA will be dispelled for harm reductionists and AA members alike, as well as for other readers. Thank you, Ernie!

My hope is that you will see just how much harm reduction there always has been in AA and will understand that harm reduction is not the enemy of addiction treatment– rather our hostility towards one another is. I also hope that you will see clearly just how much I love AA and hear my gratitude for it and its many members, even if I take exception to some members' ideas and some aspects of AA. I hope, too, that you'll hear an overall sense of gratitude to AA from the rest of the 12-Stepping harm reductionists: we all *do* love AA, enough to even challenge some things about it today – much as we do when we use the 4th Step in AA service groups to "take inventory" of what's working and what's not. In addition, we all believe strongly that there must be freedom of choice to attend 12-Step – or not - returning it to a "program of attraction rather than promotion," as Tradition 11 states. I also came across stories from 12-Stepping harm reductionists who told me they sometimes feel uncomfortable disclosing their personal abstinence status to some traditional harm reductionists - people with whom they work - who apparently have said that abstinence and 12-Step have no place in harm reduction. This news was a bit shocking to me and was particularly upsetting since the harm reductionists I know pride themselves on advocating for no-threshold access to services for everyone. So, while these folks may be well meaning, their actions are clearly not in keeping with harm reduction principles as they are: 1) potentially causing harm to people; 2) creating a threshold for a group of individuals; and 3) extremely judgmental, all of which are against the basic tenets of harm reduction.

The last thing I'd like to say here is "thank you" to all those who helped me in a variety of ways and yet these words seem more woefully insufficient than ever to express all the appreciation I feel. The amount of assistance I've had over the past six years is incredible: students and former students (Claudia, Julia, et al); family; friends and colleagues (especially Juliana and Ed) from all over the world; strangers willing to open their lives to me; and many others. I wish I could thank each of them individually, but as that is not possible, this expression of gratitude will have to suffice. I must thank a few people whose contributions were truly above and beyond and whose support made the difference between my completing the project or quitting - which I considered many times! Here we go:

To Patt Denning, who believed I was the perfect person to write this book because of my "dual citizenship" in 12-Step and harm reduction and who said that the title made her laugh out loud! Patt has been a mentor and friend, always making me feel welcome in the "New World" (to me!) of harm reduction. It was she who introduced me to several of the people interviewed here. To Alan Marlatt, who has guided me for more than a dozen years, beginning with my study of relapse prevention while a graduate student. Alan has always been open, beyond generous, kind and yet honest. To Sharon Pines, my editor, assuring that these stories and the rest of the book made some sense in their translation and transformation from contributor to tape to computer and back again. I couldn't have done this without you, Sharon! To my son, Jesse, who provided me with incredible graphics for my website, business cards, publicity cards, and particularly for the clever book covers. But most of all, just because he has always loved me no matter what I've done. And lastly, and most importantly, to my assistant Jenna Ferrara. Jenna has been a rock and this book's biggest cheerleader since she came aboard the project some four years ago after hearing me speak on harm reduction. Always available, even when her own family faced unspeakable challenges, she was always ready to do whatever it took to help me complete this project. Jenna, you are a saint!! Thank you for teaching me about the strength of the human spirit and how not to give up.

And to those of you reading this, I'd truly be grateful to hear from you regarding your thoughts, comments or feelings about this book. Please contact me through www.responsiblerecovery.org. Thank you!!

Dee-Dee Stout
May 2009
San Francisco, CA

PREFACE

"The roads to recovery are many."

- Bill Wilson, 1944, AA Grapevine (as quoted by William L. White in *"Toward a New Recovery Movement: Historical Reflections on Treatment and Advocacy,"* 2000, CSAT, p35)

One of the main reasons I felt compelled to write this book is that I, like so many other alcohol and drug counselors, wasn't taught much about harm reduction. All I learned were these two things: 1) the existence of methadone treatment, which I was taught to believe wasn't to be defined as either recovery or abstinence and 2) that harm reduction was wrong-headed because it wasn't abstinence-based. It took many years before I realized not only that these ideas were incorrect but also that they were damaging beliefs for a professional counselor and instructor in the field. One of my "a-ha" moments came in the classroom. A student asked me if I believed she was in recovery. This was a middle-aged woman, back in school for the first time in ages, working really hard in school and on methadone maintenance treatment for some 20 years. I was stunned into silence (anyone who knows me will appreciate how truly amazing that is) and, finally, after she described her life, I said: "Yes! You are working to make changes in your life; you are certainly mindful of what you are doing; and you state you have a connection to yourself and others." I surprised even myself with my answer, even though it was clearly the truth. I have had many moments such as this in the last ten years, my time of opening to the real ideas of harm reduction: that, simply put, any positive change is recovery and that all lives are worth saving.

I was privileged to enter a residential treatment facility in Oakland, California, in January 1988 after 20 years of drinking and drugging to cover a lot of pain and to seek acceptance and popularity. It worked – for a long while. And when it stopped working, it was horrible. My ex-husband paid for my treatment as it was he who kept insisting that I do something about my drinking (he didn't know of my other drug use for years). I first went to an AA meeting at his insistence and hated every minute of it. But after treatment, things were different: I realized what I had to lose (my son and husband) and even began to see that I might be worth saving. I had a wonderful counselor who saw how much pain I was in and was gentle with me. However, the AA that I went into was not so gentle. I saw and heard some terrible things over the many years I attended meetings (including some abroad). But I was also honored to work with, and then be sponsored by, the Drs. Marsh: Mickey and Earle.

Mickey Apter-Marsh had a PhD in Human Sexuality, which is how she had met Dr. Earle (he was a colleague of Alfred Kinsey and the former Chair of the OB-GYN department at the University of California, San Francisco). Those two were amazing and wonderful! Earle had written a chapter in the second edition of the *Big Book* of AA called "Physician, Heal Thyself" and was a friend of Bill Wilson (co-founder of AA and Earle's sponsor) and told me wonderful stories of Bill and the old AA. He told me of an AA that I often didn't see in meetings but saw in some of the people who attended meetings, and so it was the AA of the book (third edition at that time) that I came to love.

Another book I loved at that time was a little paperback called *Came to Believe.* This book was a collection of stories of some members of AA who wrote paragraphs or pages on how they had come to believe in a higher power. It didn't lecture or recite facts. All it offered were the experiences of several members in their own voices. I loved that book. When I envisioned writing this book that is the book that came to mind, and its style is what I wanted to emulate. While are many well-written books on the principles and practice of harm reduction, there's nothing that tells us anything about how to make the culture shift from total abstinence-based thinking to a more encompassing theory and practice. That's what

I am hoping to accomplish with this book. And, as we're a culture of stories, and stories are often the catalyst for change, I wanted simply to allow the voices of those of us who had already made this culture shift to be heard. In treatment, we often suggest looking to those who do not have problems with behaviors as role models for what to do rather than always emphasizing what not to do. Here, I offer the voices of those professionals who have always been on the side of any positive change so that you can hear clearly how and why they did not become part of the majority abstinence-only culture.

Finally, I felt I had to write this book after I became quite ill and disabled with a chronic condition. Struggling with decisions around who I was and what decisions to make, I found myself forced to look outside of meetings for help and to other paradigms of health, such as *harm reduction*. As I was beginning to ask questions of Dr. Earle and others, I found myself seeking answers from some new people to my life. The first of these was Alan Marlatt, due to my interest in relapse prevention, and then there were Jeannie Little and Patt Denning. Along the road others such as Bill Miller (the man who brought us Motivational Interviewing) and Scott Miller, Jane Peller, and John Walters came into my life. Their teachings, and their acceptance of me and my struggles to just be, were critical in expanding my thinking about behavior change and addiction. It is these learnings, these new ways of being with clients, that I wanted to share through this collection of voices and extraordinary ideas.

While talking to the incredible clinicians and other health professionals whose voices you'll be hearing in this book, I was struck by several recurring themes. One is how these practitioners/professionals had to think "out of the box" when they began to see people with difficult addiction issues, often involving "co-occurring disorders." while treating these clients, the workers felt that using harm reduction principles and strategies was a no-brainer, and this decision, happily, led to much success. And as these practitioners are smarter than your average bear, those successes, no matter how small, led them to keep doing more of what was working well with clients. Sometimes those strategies included 12-Step but, just as often, it did not. It was completely up to the client to decide. Which leads us to another recurring theme: when clients chose their own goals and methods - with respectful practitioner feedback - they seemed to have more successful outcomes, more often than not. It begs the question, why do we continue to insist on being the experts on individual change when clearly clients are the experts on their own lives, and typically have specific ideas about how to change (Scott Miller and Barry Duncan call this the clients' *theory of change*[2]) that could help them successfully make changes?

A third theme you will hear throughout all the stories is that of *Motivational Interviewing*[3], or MI. MI was first described in an article written in 1983 by Dr. William Miller, Distinguished Professor Emeritus in the department of Psychology and Research at the University of New Mexico, Albuquerque (Dr. Miller's story can be found in the Oldtimers' section). At its core, MI is a way of being with people that includes these four guiding principles: 1) expressing empathy towards clients and their situations; 2) working to help clients acknowledge the discrepancies in their lives (how their current behavior fits with their values and goals in life); 3) rolling with the natural resistance all persons have toward change; and 4) helping support a client's self-efficacy. In MI, these four principles are accomplished through: 1) collaborating with clients to help them formulate their goals and the methods to obtain them (called the "menu of options"), 2) eliciting ideas from clients about change and providing feedback with permission on those ideas and 3) acknowledging and supporting a client's autonomy and choices. We call these principles the *foundation of Spirit* in MI and, in combination with the skills and strategies that put the principles into action, we have the entire musical score of MI. Even now, MI's goal-oriented method of conversation is unique both in addiction treatment and in many other forms of health behavior change treatment. Some researchers and practitioners have stated that MI is the most important contribution to effecting behavior change since AA came on the scene. With its collaborative and goal-oriented methods, MI could be a bridge between harm reduction and some of the old treatment models. Ultimately, both AA and MI are about making changes in one's life, in much the same way that I and others in the field have advocated for a change in culture in addiction treatment.

My voice and the other voices that will speak to you from these pages aren't the only ones that are calling for change. There are other key people in the field who are advocating for a new paradigm. The eminent author and historian, William White, author of *Slaying the Dragon*[4] states that it is indeed time to redefine recovery and even sobriety. I couldn't agree more. According to Mr. White, recovery can mean complete abstinence from drug - including alcohol - use and other health behaviors, but it can also mean reducing the use of drugs and other less than healthy behaviors. Furthermore, he states that AA realized this from the beginning, which is why it did not close the door on those who inevitably relapsed: "*progress not perfection.*" And this realization meant recognizing that this "recovery from addiction" would take many forms, all of which were valid.

He goes on to suggest that the current recovery movement will need to address such "contentious issues" as how harm reduction interventions might play a role in traditional treatment and recovery and where long-term methadone maintenance clients fit in a new definition of recovery (we would say it belongs right smack in the middle of it, pardon the pun!). White believes that these issues, especially the concept of re-defining recovery and sobriety, are crucial for the long-term health of the recovery movement. In fact, he raises doubts as to the movement's ability to remain vital without significant change and unity, including the acceptance of all recovery organizations and individual practices as potentially being viable to the recovery of an individual.

So here we are, at the beginning of this book - perhaps at the beginning of a new movement: a movement that warmly welcomes any positive change. What would recovery and treatment be like if we really did focus only on the outcome - *the change that someone wants to make* – and let go completely of the road to that change? I believe this would be the recovery and treatment that Bill Wilson and Dr. Bob (and others) imagined: real treatment, real recovery, as each person can and wants to make it for their own lives – true freedom. There are many of us who still believe this is possible and work to make it happen. You're about to meet some of them.

But first, let's have a discussion about the language of harm reduction and recovery.

WHAT IS THIS THING CALLED HARM REDUCTION?

"RECOVERY"

I think that defining terms is a good way to begin our discussion of harm reduction. It seems that what often gets us into hot water is not having agreed-upon working definitions of terms before launching a serious conversation. Without that prior consensus, we can wind up talking *at* each other rather than *to* each other. So, to avoid this scenario here, I went looking for definitions to get things off on the right footing. Since both 12-Steppers and harm reductionists state that they work to support people towards recovery and since "recovery" has been used in AA circles in a manner that seemingly excludes "harm reduction," I think that going back in history to seek out a definition of recovery and re-examining some misinterpretations of harm reduction are important first steps in this discussion.

    Since "recovery" is a word used so often these days (see any supermarket tabloid or read almost any autobiography!), you would think that finding a definition in the standard AA or other addiction texts would be easy. It proved to be a task, however, that was definitely more complicated than I had imagined, and even more interesting for what I did *not* find than for what I did. Here are my (few) discoveries in the search for definitions of recovery and, by the way, nearly all the books I looked through on the subject of addiction and treatment – numbering more than 20 – had no definition at all!

In one source, *Ad-dic-tion-ary* (Wilson & Wilson, Hazelden, 1992), a once-popular book still used by some addiction certification schools and many others in the field, the term "recovery" is described as "a *journey*, not a *destination* (italics theirs)." The authors, however, fail to provide a more specific definition. What is the journey? What is the destination? It seems this is all left up to the reader. The authors do *not* state, though, that attending 12-Step meetings, working the 12-Steps, or even being abstinent defines recovery. They only say that recovery "is a threat to your addiction…[and] reading this manual is evidence that [your] recovery has already begun…."(p. 283)

I did not find the word "recovery" used at all in the book, *Alcoholics Anonymous*[5]. The closest it comes is using the term "recovering" twice, and then only in the 3rd Edition. The first instance is found in the footnote on page 104: "…whether she is still drinking or is *recovering* in AA (italics mine)." The second time it's used is found in "Chapter 9: The Family Afterward," which begins by saying: "Our women folk have suggested certain attitudes a wife may take with the husband who is *recovering* (again, italics mine)." Neither of these uses of the term really helps us pin down a clear definition of the word, however, and several uses of the term "recovered" also offer no assistance in this regard.

[Aside: I wonder if this seemingly surprising lack of use of the term "recovery" or "recovered" in addiction literature might have a lot to do with the fact that addiction professionals, theorists, and much of the current 12-Step thinking all believe addiction to be a chronic, relapsing disorder and, when awakened like a sleeping tiger, is something to be feared, leading inevitably to "jails, institutions, or death."[6] We must be vigilant in not allowing this tiger to awaken; therefore, this is one disease from which we never fully "recover" (read *become cured*). However, in not using the term "recovered," we also imply that treatment does not work, that addicts are never able to get beyond being only former addicts, i.e. "once a pickle, never again a cucumber," as the old saying goes.]

Turning to the dictionary (or its postmodern equivalent: www.dictionary.com), we find our only detailed definition [Author's note: a look at other dictionaries uncovered similar definitions]. Recovery is defined here as:

An act of recovering
  a. *The regaining of or possibility of regaining something lost or taken away.*
  b. *Restoration or return to health from sickness.*
  c. *Restoration or return to any former and better state or condition.*

Note that nowhere in this definition is recovery necessarily and inextricably linked to the words "12-Step" or even "abstinence." What the dictionary does indicate is that the most consistent aspect of recovery is this: *a restoration or return to health*.

Patt Denning, in her book *Practicing Harm Reduction Psychotherapy* (The Guilford Press, 2002), discusses the use of the term "recovery," and what she says is relevant in terms of our dictionary definition. She writes that Alcoholics Anonymous appropriated the word to apply only to people who are attending 12-Step meetings for help with an addiction and who are seeking abstinence[7]. I would add that most treatment agencies use the term in this way as well. Think about it: when someone says they are "in recovery" culturally we certainly think of 12-Step and abstinence, right? Just watch any television show with a "recovering" character. Have you ever seen someone *not* talk about the 12-Steps and being abstinent if they described themselves as "recovering?" No. Again, I think this appropriation of the term plays into the false dichotomy between 12-Steppers and harm reductionists and facilitates the mistaken belief that abstinence (via 12-Step) is the only way to recover. But is 12-Step really the only way to recover? Was it ever intended to be? We'll look at that point later in the chapter on the history and development of Alcoholics Anonymous.

At this point, what we can see is that the dictionary definition of "recovery," in emphasizing turning away from sickness and moving towards health, would most certainly allow us to place a whole spectrum of strategies and actions within the concept of recovery. In fact, the very definition implies dynamism: "the act of recovering", "regaining", "returning to" -- a focus on process that is much broader than merely defining recovery as a preoccupation with abstinence (as Dr. Denning alludes to). We'll see that the theory and practice of harm reduction fits right into this notion of movement and process towards a healthier state.

Dee-Dee Stout

"HARM REDUCTION"

Over the years, there has been a lot of misunderstanding about harm reduction, along with many distracting and wrong-headed myths concerning its principles and practice, which have led directly to much of the controversy surrounding it. Sometimes people have simply misinterpreted or inaccurately stated the goals or ethics of the agencies, municipalities, or people implementing some aspects of harm reduction policy. Often, however, these misunderstandings have led to core challenges of harm reduction policies by those who advocate for abstinence-only treatment for addictions. Since transparency is a major point of harm reduction policy, let me shed a little sunshine on some of these controversies and misinterpretations while developing a working definition of harm reduction as I go along.

Myth #1: Harm reduction is the opposite of abstinence.

Abstinence is and always has been one of the possible outcomes of harm reduction treatment. Abstinence is found on the continuum of drug use used in harm reduction theory and practice[8], although one could accurately say it's on *one* end of a continuum and is one possibility in a menu of outcome options a client might choose. In fact, it could be argued that harm reduction puts abstinence in perspective and sees how it may not be the right fit for everyone. You might look at it this way: *abstinence from anything equals perfection*. As we are human and, therefore, by definition imperfect, the much-observed inability to be perfectly abstinent (the tendency to relapse or slip) often leads us to feeling shameful when we inevitably behave as a human being does: i.e., we *make a mistake*. And, ironically, the shame we feel as a result of not being able to maintain anything like "perfect adherence"[9] to this desired outcome of abstinence often leads us right back to the behavior we're trying to avoid or stop (see Alan Marlatt's discussion of the *AVE*: the abstinence violation effect in his seminal book *Relapse Prevention*[10]).

Back in early AA, this idea of perfection was a topic that was often discussed. In fact, this concern led the early groups to embrace those who slipped - i.e., drank - in order to help reduce the shame lapsed members often felt, as everyone recognized no one among them was perfect. Coming to the aid of a lapsed member was also thought to help other members avoid the pitfalls that had led to that member's slip; it was seen as a learning opportunity for all members. This was when the AA slogan "progress not perfection" started to be heard.

Our definition of harm reduction, therefore, begins with the premise that there is a menu of options, including abstinence, available to those seeking help or in treatment, and only they alone can ultimately make the choice to abstain or to moderate – or to continue their behavior, whatever that may be. Harm reduction, along with AA as described above, clearly recognizes in its notion of choice that no one is perfect and therefore attempts to build-in a process towards health (recovery) that is personal, appropriate, and shame-reducing (think AVE) when less-than-perfect behavior occurs. Harm reduction also believes that people make their own choices best after getting accurate and impartial information on all the possible options available to them, including the pros and cons of each, and various supports available. With this, people will have all they need to make better, more informed decisions.

Myth #2: Clinicians should be in charge of treatment, not clients.

Typically, we think of treatment as a group of professionals or an agency making decisions for clients based on the beliefs that 1) clients can't make healthy decisions for themselves ("your best thinking got you here") and 2) we're the experts, so we logically know how best to treat this condition(s). But are these beliefs true? We harm reductionists would say "not necessarily." We would certainly agree that there are occasions when folks might need additional help in their decision-making processes, and we'd even agree that occasionally someone might be so ill (perhaps a methamphetamine psychosis) that a single decision might need to be made for them in the moment. We would, however, strongly disagree with those who say we must make *all* decisions for all drug users as long as they're using. Why do we disagree? Well, because we *do* believe that their best thinking got them "here" - to us! People often come to treatment under the influence of drugs, and we'd all say that was a healthy decision, right?

Also, we know that different drugs interact with each individual user differently [Author's note: see the 1984 book *Drug, Set,*

Setting by Norman Zinberg, Yale University Press, for more]. Therefore, we must form professional opinions and policies based on the individual in front of us, on his or her behavior and on his or her goals – not on the particular drug of choice (for example, a bad policy based on inaccurate information might be one that states "all heroin users are incapable of rational decision making so they need extended structured residential treatment dictated by treatment professionals."). Good policy looks at the whole relationship of the individual to drug(s) use: the individual's history, physiology, the context of use, the particular drug and how it's being used plus the desired outcome or goals of the individual. In other words, all decisions regarding treatment options must be individualized and personalized. So good policy might say, "Since you have a family who cares, a desire to stop using heroin and work you enjoy, what do *you* think would be useful to help you stay stopped?" And if I felt that as a professional I wanted to share my thoughts with this client, I would merely ask to do so: "I wonder if I could share some of my ideas for treatment possibilities that I think could help you make this decision?" Most people are more than happy to hear our opinions; they simply want to be respected for having their own as well. Therefore, to extend our developing definition of harm reduction and to counter Myth #2, we harm reductionists would all say that respecting the opinions and choices (including the choice to be abstinent) of the individual seeking help is always the most important aspect of harm reduction theory and practice.

Myth #3: Harm reduction is just giving people permission to use.

OK, this is the Big One. And the smart-aleck response from me is this: personally, never *ever* in 20 years of using various drugs did I ask *anybody* for permission to use *anything*, so this statement is completely meaningless. And that's the truth. Whenever I've asked other former or current users – or just a regular Joe or Jane - if they've ever asked permission from someone before they've used a drug of any kind, I've never received an affirmative response. But let me not be a smart aleck and, instead, let's discuss this issue a bit further, as I do think it's an important point.

This idea of "giving permission" implies that I somehow *can* give permission to another person. But as a human being, I can neither give nor take permission from another human being. First of all, it's simply not literally possible: how would I do such a thing? I might believe that I have such power in some way but, in reality, that is a sham. Now what I might have is *leverage*, which is different. The difference is this: *power* implies that I, through my own desires, can make you do something. *Leverage* means that I can threaten or cajole you into something, such as making a change. Very different. For instance, to use an example in the context of the criminal justice system, I can send people to jail, or back to jail, or away from their families, but how can I be sure that they will show up at jail as opposed to running off or, on another note, how could I really make sure they never used drugs again? I can't be with them all the time, and drug tests only tell me what someone *might* have done (past tense) not what they're doing right now, so that's not really a helpful measurement in this case. Leverage goes only so far even in a coercive system such as criminal justice.

What that means is that there must be some buy-in from the users, some agreement on their part in order for them to go to get help. Harm reduction approaches have actually been shown to increase the motivation toward change (including towards abstinence) for users, often even more than traditional treatment approaches, in part through the addition of that personal buy-in [Editor's note: see the book *Motivational Interviewing*, 2nd Edition (Miller and Rollnick, The Guilford Press) for more on this phenomena]. Isn't that remarkable? And you know, when left with the choice to be abstinent or moderate in their drinking, most people eventually seem to decide to be abstinent – on their own. Colleagues and I have compared notes, and we find that clients often say that abstinence is just easier than trying to moderate and keep track of your drinks, or that it isn't nearly as much fun if you can't get drunk (yes, responsible drinking means not getting drunk – ever!). In general, we see that people naturally want to be healthier; it's just that we're so darned hard-wired not to like change that we try to avoid it sometimes even when we really know it's what's best. And by the way, that's not denying the need for change – or being in denial - that's just being human!

So, in shattering Myth #3, we include in our growing definition of harm reduction the fact that, far from giving people permission to use, harm reductionists help uncover the internal motivations in people and support their natural instinct towards healthier, and even abstinent, behavior. This includes exploring the motivations of people's behavior through posing some challenging questions and using artful reflections to help people come to terms with the discrepancies in the realities of their lives – not in a harsh way but in an honest way: how is their current behavior(s) helping or hindering them from getting the goals they want in life?

Myth#4: You can't mix harm reduction and abstinence goals in treatment/harm reduction means that anything goes.

I thought I would combine these last two as I think they are related. First of all, I've often heard that we can't mix goals in treatment: clients who want to abstain will be triggered by those who do not or who are under-the-influence in the meeting. I've also heard consistently that there are liability issues for agencies, which is why they don't allow anyone who is under the influence of drugs to be on the premises, client or not.

Realistically, if you walk into almost any 12-Step meeting at anytime, you're likely to sit next to someone who is under the influence of some drug, including alcohol. And, amazingly, no one tells them to leave, and no one gets upset that they're being "triggered," in spite of the abstinence-only message many receive in 12-Step meetings. In fact, members are often the kindest to those who come to meetings under the influence (perhaps we're reminded of where we came from - and where we could be again?). Sometimes the secretary of the meeting will suggest – *not insist* – that this person might just want to listen at that day's meeting instead of speaking but, mostly, that person would simply be invited to "Keep Coming Back!"

As for the oft-repeated statement that harm reduction means "anything goes," that there is no structure to harm reduction-based treatment, I offer the following thoughts. Harm reduction psychotherapy is a complicated combination of accurate education, different therapeutic models, medications, skill building, nutrition, support from family and concerned others, and more. It is as comprehensive a treatment as any I know. Again, it is a long held myth than harm reduction simply means the client does whatever they want, with no consequence. No harm reductionist would want someone to drive a car under the influence of a drug that could impair their ability to safely navigate a road. But we might advocate for treatment over jail time. We always hold people responsible for their actions. In fact, that is the very point: we harm reductionists don't care as much about what or how someone uses a drug as we care about **how you behave under its influence**. So, far from being an "anything goes" policy or treatment approach, harm reduction is the *gold-standard* for holding people accountable. So, what does this look like in an agency setting?

Good question. As harm reduction is all about *reducing* harm not increasing it, we agree that facilities, agencies, workers and policy makers need guidelines - just not as many as we all may think we need. Guidelines - safety tenets, rules, whatever you may call them – aren't reasons for unilateral prohibitions such as discharging clients who use drugs or engage in other behaviors that led them to treatment. Let's say that again: we should not discharge clients *for exhibiting the very behavior(s) for which they are in treatment*! Substance abuse and/or dependence is a mental health condition; it's found in the DSM-IV-TR, the guidebook for mental health conditions and substance use disorders. So how has it happened that substance use disorders get viewed differently from other disorders or medical conditions? How is it that treatment for this set of illnesses – substance use disorders - does not allow people to show any visible *signs* of their illness (using drugs, resisting treatment options, ambivalence about making changes, yelling at staff, etc.) if they want to get treatment? Think about it: if you were having heart problems and you came to the emergency room in the midst of a heart attack, would someone suggest that you needed to just stop and "come back when you're really ready to stop having heart attacks and take this seriously," which might include giving up your job, your home, your family, and more in order to just *get help*, because we're not even talking about solving the problem here yet. Furthermore, once individuals do decide to enter treatment of some kind and change their relationship to drugs, if their symptoms return, why is it that, instead of looking at the *treatment* as possibly being ineffective, we instead so often first blame and punish the 'patients/clients' by discharging them, withholding treatments, punishing them, or labeling them as "resistant," "antisocial/borderline," "in denial" or worse? And more importantly, how is this *not* completely unethical behavior on our part?

So, to integrate these concepts into our definition, we can see that, far from a philosophy of "anything goes," harm reduction is dedicated to treating an individual regardless of where on the spectrum of use (or change) that person is and does not withhold treatment based on some fixed and predetermined judgment having nothing to do with the unique circumstances of that individual. The final piece of our harm reduction definition, then, involves an ethical and compassionate acceptance of the whole person combined with a collaborative approach whose goal is to help individuals improve their lives, however they would define that, one step at a time.

Ultimately, our discussion of definitions and myths comes down to beliefs. Terence Gorski, in his booklet *Mistaken Beliefs*[11], defines mistaken beliefs as things that people believe to be true and therefore act as if they are when in fact, the beliefs are false. He says that acting as if these beliefs are true is likely to cause problems to an individual user and, therefore, is to be guarded against, especially in early recovery. I believe that we, as members of our profession, have been acting as if these mistaken beliefs about harm reduction - the myths we've been discussing - are true rather than challenging them by seeking out accurate information. In 12-Step language, I could say we have been "looking at the differences rather than the similarities," which any 12-Stepper knows is not what 12-Step advocates. And, bottom line, the health of people with addictions is far too important to continue acting out these differences amongst ourselves or on our clients. So I'm going to stop here with a saying that I find bridges these worlds of 12-Step and harm reduction – again, mistakenly seen as opposite ideas all too often - and one on which I believe we can all agree: "Recovery is any positive change," and we all want to help people make positive changes in their lives. What I think I love most about this phrase is that it was first spoken, not by my harm reductionist friend and colleague Dan Bigg (Chicago Recovery Alliance) as I had once thought, but rather by a 12-Step loving, regular meeting-attending, heroin-using gentle man named John Szyler, aka "Division Street." John died of an overdose in May 1996 but not before giving us these few extraordinary words: "Recovery is any positive change." I hope his legacy will be to not be known only as a drug user, but rather as a visionary who happened to use drugs sometimes, who helped us come together as professionals and concerned others who care deeply about our fellow humans who may also be drug users; and also as someone who aided us in our desire to stop letting these "outside issues," as AA might call this feud, interfere with what our hearts all know is true: *that all lives are indeed worth saving,* and that *any positive change* is the way to do it. Lastly, perhaps this conversation, rather than controversy and debate, could continue if we were to take to heart this quote from Johann Wolfgang von Goethe, the German writer and philosopher: *"Treat people as if they are what they can be, and you help them to become who they're capable of being."* And that is *my* definition of harm reduction.

WILL THE REAL AA PLEASE STAND UP?

A BRIEF HISTORY OF HARM REDUCTION IN AA

So, how did we arrive at such a basic disagreement in our field? What happened in the history of addiction treatment that led to the belief that there exists a vast chasm between the 12-Step model and the public health principles of the harm reduction approach? How did Alcoholics Anonymous and the 12-Step movement, originally full of harm reduction concepts, move toward more dogma and less tolerance? Here, I hope to show how harm reduction echoes throughout the original writings of AA, how and why the 12-Step movement and AA left much of its harm reduction roots behind and how this movement, adopting the disease model approach along the way, became the predominant alcohol and drug treatment paradigm in the United States.

Alcoholics Anonymous, or AA, was born in blue collar America in 1935, six years after the stock market crash of 1929 in the midst of the Great Depression. It was founded by two compulsive, heavy drinkers who were at the end of their ropes (as were their wives and friends) due to their shared inability to find successful treatment of any kind to help them stop. They were: William (Bill) Griffith Wilson, a denizen of Wall street, and Dr. Robert (Dr. Bob) Holbrook Smith, a graduate of Rush Medical School in Chicago and a physician, who met Bill Wilson at the home of Henrietta Seiberling in Akron, Ohio, a meeting that led to the creation of the basic concepts that became Alcoholics Anonymous, the most well-known self-help organization in the world.

To better understand how an initial orientation toward harm reduction in AA was lost and describe the differences between the original AA and AA today - and to better appreciate what's happened to AA as a whole - we need to go back and take a look at the evolution of AA in the context of the history of alcohol use and abuse in the United States during AA's early years. And here Ernie Kurtz, PhD, often considered the preeminent expert on the history of AA, shall guide us. Since Dr. Kurtz has already provided us with an authoritative history of AA in his book *Not-God* (Hazelden, 1991), we will focus on the relevant historical aspects of the early recovery movement within the greater American culture.

At the turn of the 20th century, the moderate Temperance Movement became the more zealous Abstinence Movement, culminating in the passage of the 18th Amendment on January 29, 1919. Prohibitionists believed that all our social problems stemmed from "demon rum" and other types of alcohol. They truly believed that eliminating alcohol would lead to the elimination of poverty, domestic violence and other problems of the time. Prohibition would last for thirteen years, during which time violent crime and other social ills would increase as organized crime became the distribution hub for alcohol, especially higher-proof alcohol due to its greater profitability for the likes of Al Capone. For all its good intentions, sadly, the "noble experiment" of Prohibition would mostly fail (although alcohol-related family violence would decrease as would death by cirrhosis) in its attempts to rein in alcohol consumption. It, and its supporters, would go down in history as the single greatest reason for the increase in the rates of alcohol consumption and related problems.

The results of [Prohibition] clearly indicate that it was a miserable failure on all counts...The lessons of Prohibition remain important today. They apply not only to the debate over the war on drugs but also to the mounting efforts to drastically reduce access to alcohol and tobacco and to such issues as censorship and bans on insider trading, abortion, and gambling. Although consumption of alcohol fell at the beginning of Prohibition, it subsequently increased. Alcohol became more dangerous to consume; crime increased and became "organized"; the court and prison systems were stretched to the breaking point; and corruption of public officials was rampant. No measurable gains were made in productivity or reduced absenteeism. Prohibition removed a significant source of tax revenue and greatly increased government spending. It led many drinkers to switch to opium, marijuana, patent medicines, cocaine, and other dangerous substances that they would have been unlikely to encounter in the absence of Prohibition.[12]

Here is another view, as stated by industrialist and prohibitionist John D. Rockefeller in a letter dated 1932:

"When Prohibition was introduced, I hoped that it would be widely supported by public opinion and the day would soon come when the evil effects of alcohol would be recognized. I have slowly and reluctantly come to believe that this has not been the result. Instead, drinking has generally increased; the speakeasy has replaced the saloon; a vast army of lawbreakers has appeared; many of our best citizens have openly ignored Prohibition; respect for the law has been greatly lessened; and crime has increased to a level never seen before."[13]

So here's where we've arrived as a country around 1935: we tried to outlaw alcohol but that didn't work; in fact, now some things are worse (organized crime). We seem able to admit and accept that Prohibition has been a disaster, but we don't really know where to go or what to do next. We also tried experiments such as 3.2% beer (with the passage of the 18th Amendment in March 1933). But that doesn't go over well either: it seems people want their wine and beer with full alcohol content. We've also come to the conclusion that since we all can't agree on what we should do about alcohol, we'll let each state make its own laws[14] – which leads to a patchwork quilt of various "dry" and "wet" states! And, of course, in the midst of all this emphasis on alcohol, we need also remember that the country was in the greatest economic crisis ever recorded: the Great Depression.

Some believe the Great Depression began with Black Tuesday: October 29, 1929, the day the stock market crashed. Even if the Great Depression was not caused by Black Tuesday, to one formerly successful stockbroker in New York City by the name of Bill Wilson, this was a devastating time. So, is it any wonder that "demon alcohol" became Bill W.'s good friend, as it did to many others? It was also during this time that Bill would periodically seek help for his ever-increasing drinking as it become more and more uncontrollable and he became more unpredictable, culminating in three hospitalizations under the care of Dr. William Silkworth[15]. And since "drunkenness was condemned and punished, but only as an abuse of a God-given gift. Drink itself was not looked upon as culpable, any more than food deserved blame for the sin of gluttony. Excess was a personal indiscretion,"[16] it seems logical that American problem drinkers like Bill would come together to seek a spiritual solution to their drinking troubles. This spiritual solution or awakening would become the most important aspect of AA and would shape the final comments of the final speech (in 1970) Bill W. would make in his beloved AA before his death[17]. It also echoes the only promise that AA would ever make: "Having had a spiritual awakening as *the* result of these Steps, we tried to carry this message to alcoholics and to practice these principles in all our affairs (Step 12; emphasis mine)."[18] Here is part of a passage from *Not-God*,[19] quoting Bill Wilson, from Robert Thomsen's "Bill W:"

"...*Deflation at depth*, yes, that was *it*.... My thoughts began to race as I envisioned a chain reaction among alcoholics, one carrying this message and these principles to the next. More than I could ever want anything else, I now knew that I wanted to work with other alcoholics." (emphasis his)

It was during this time in early 1935 that Bill Wilson received guidance from an old friend, Ebby T. (Ebby would become Bill's first sponsor). Ebby had found sobriety (though short-lived) through the evangelical Christian fellowship, the Oxford Group (it was partly due to this early association with The Oxford Group that Bill would later write the concepts that became the Twelve Steps). The Oxford Group, however, was too strict and proselytized too much for either Bill or Dr. Bob, who had joined Bill by now. Bill and Dr. Bob also began to have discussions about alcoholism with Dr. William Silkworth, who had been instrumental in Bill's recovery during his last drinking episode (in late 1934) when once again, he found himself at Silkworth's Town's Hospital. These conversations with Silkworth, combined with Bill and Bob's own experiences with alcohol, led these three men to the conclusion that alcoholism was an allergy and those who suffered from it should not be treated as sinners, but rather as ill with obsession and compulsion.

And so, Alcoholics Anonymous officially began as a way to help support men who were trying to stop drinking. Its early members were much like Dr. Bob and Bill W.: middle-class white men who were desperate - severely alcohol dependent – for whom nothing else had worked. And they had tried everything. The original AA, as described in the main texts of AA - the books Alcoholics Anonymous, known as the Big Book by its members, and the Twelve Steps and Twelve Traditions (known to AA members as the "12 by 12" or "12 and 12") from which the 12-Step phenomenon got its name - believed that people had to decide for themselves if they were alcoholic or not; no one was labeled or forced to label themselves or to attend or speak in meetings[20]. Members were typically recruited only after several unsuccessful attempts at controlled drinking, losing their family and jobs and various forms of unsuccessful treatments including hospitalizations (most new members heard about AA after a hospital visit from Bill W. or other members): in other words, after "hitting bottom."

There was no negativity towards any man who could "drink like a gentleman"[21] or who decided not to return for whatever reason. Men who were drunk were welcomed into these meetings and sat next to those who were sober. In meetings, one talked about anything he (and later she) felt was needed to stay sober, because AA believed that drinking was merely a symptom of a greater underlying spiritual problem, and members who worked the 12-Steps were given a "daily reprieve contingent on the maintenance of [that] spiritual condition."[22] Everything was related to drinking. No one was asked if they were "sincere"[23] in their desire to stop drinking[24] or if that desire would last longer than the usual hour and a half meeting. In other words, AA was originally completely harm reductionistic – even *with* its ultimate goal of abstinence. Why? Because it stressed that the goal – abstinence or controlled drinking - was up to the *individual*, not AA or anyone else, and that is the core of all harm reduction practices. One expression of this core value of AA can be found everywhere in AA meetings: "take what you want and leave the rest."

So, how does AA define an alcoholic? Surprisingly, according to the book *Alcoholics Anonymous*, not everyone who uses alcohol, or even has trouble with alcohol, is considered an alcoholic - very harm reductionistic! In *More About Alcoholism*[25], we find quite a bit of information about how the original AA distinguished between who was an alcoholic and who was not. Here is one example:

"We admit we have some of these symptoms, but we have not gone to the extremes you fellows did, nor are we likely to, for we understand ourselves so well after what you have told us that such things cannot happen again. We have not lost everything in life through drinking and we certainly do not intend to.

That may be true of certain nonalcoholic people who, though drinking foolishly and heavily at the present time, are able to stop or moderate, because their brains and bodies have not been damaged as ours were. But the actual or potential alcoholic, with hardly an exception, will be absolutely unable to stop drinking on the basis of self-knowledge."

There are numerous other examples of harm reduction - more than I can completely cover here - found in both the main text, *Alcoholics Anonymous*, and in *Twelve Steps and Twelve Traditions*. Here are some other examples of harm reduction in AA to give you the general idea of just how much harm reduction – read *tolerance* - there really is in AA as originally conceived:

> 1. The Slogans -– or "bumper sticker therapy" as some call these – display a tangible sense of inclusion, welcome and non-judgment: *Live and Let Live; Keep Coming Back; Attraction Rather Than Promotion; Principles before Personalities; First Things First; Keep an Open Mind; Keep It Simple; Fake It till you Make It; One Day at a Time!*[26]
>
> 2. The following quotes are indicative of the lack of prescriptiveness:
>
> - "Our book is meant to be suggestive only."[27]
>
> - "You will be most successful with alcoholics if you *do not exhibit any passion* for crusade or reform. *Never talk down* to an alcoholic from any moral or spiritual hilltop; simply lay out the kit of spiritual tools for his inspection. Show him how they worked with you. *Offer him friendship and fellowship*. Tell him that if he wants to get well you will do anything to help…*He should not be pushed or prodded* by you, his wife, or his friends… If he thinks he can do the job in some other way, or prefers some other spiritual approach, *encourage him to follow his own conscience. We have no monopoly* on God; we merely have an approach that worked with us…

Let it go at that."[28] (emphasis mine)
- "Here are the steps we took which are *suggested* as a program of recovery." (emphasis mine)

And this quote that clearly allows for a graduated approach to the problem of drink:

"People have said we must not go where liquor is served; we must not have it in our homes; we must shun friends who drink; we must avoid moving picture which show drinking scenes; we must not go into bars; our friends must hide their bottles if we go to their houses; we mustn't think or be reminded about alcohol at all...In our belief any scheme of combating alcoholism which proposes to shield the sick man from temptation is doomed to failure."[29]

Finally, it is interesting that Bill Wilson never expected people to live their entire lives in AA; the point of AA, he said, was to help a person return to society and their lives, according to his longtime friend and sponsee, Dr. Earle Marsh ("Doc Earle")[30]. In fact, on occasion, Bill W. would state the only reason he continued to attend meetings was because he felt obligated. It's what members and others expected of him.

Let's now look at how things have changed. First of all, let's consider AA meetings. Are there differences between how meetings were conducted in the early beginnings of AA and how they work now? Well, just as in those early meetings, if you were to walk into most[31] meetings drunk today, someone would likely suggest that you not speak in the meeting, but instead would suggest that you just listen in order not to disturb the meeting and to truly see if AA is for you. Then, as now, you'd be likely to hear, "Just keep coming back, friend!" In many other respects, however, you might not recognize today's AA.

On the positive side, today you will see all sexualities/genders, people from many countries speaking many languages, teenagers, interested family and friends, professionals - even reporters - and many others at a typical open[32] AA meeting – either attending for themselves or to seek help in understanding what those close to them are going through. On the other hand, one of the most controversial changes you would see today is the presence of people who are required to attend AA by courts, treatment centers, parents and partners, therapists or others. This requirement nearly split AA to its very core in the 1980's when mandating attendance at AA, or other 12-Step groups, became commonplace.

Mandating AA attendance fundamentally violates Tradition 11[33] whose principle of attraction rather than promotion is a core AA value. In addition, required attendance would seem to violate Tradition 4[34], which states that each separate AA group should be autonomous, except in matters affecting other groups or AA as a whole. When the influx of mandated attendees began in the 1980's, many in AA were upset due to this sign of disrespect – whether intentional or not - of the very traditions that, even today, are in place to keep AA open and safe for all who want to attend. Particularly important is the concept of anonymity. And yet, due to AA's tradition of having "no opinions on outside issues[35]" and a desire to support anyone who might be there for help, most of us kept silent - except in service meetings[36] - and reluctantly signed the attendance forms required by the mandated authority. Required attendance remains controversial and is still discussed in service meetings today as well as in courtrooms across the country[37].

Another controversial change is in the basic democratic structure of AA. Certain people have been employed by AA throughout its history to assist with service needs in adherence to the following AA tradition:

"Alcoholics Anonymous should remain forever nonprofessional, but our service centers may employ special workers."[38] *Tradition* 8

AA members and AA meetings, however, are actually in charge of how the organization functions through a voting process held at meetings called "taking a group conscience." The group conscience is a systematic way of asking how the individual members - and the group as a whole - feel about a certain subject, such as a new pamphlet being considered for publication. It is through the taking of this "group conscience" that AA's General Service Organization (GSO) makes all its decisions on anything affecting AA as a whole (individual groups make decisions through the same process for things affecting only that individual group, such as refreshments, the type of meeting, or the election of a new secretary).

What has been clear throughout the history of AA is that *no one speaks for AA as a whole, no matter what they may say* (this rule even extended to Bill W.).

In fact, during the last years of his life, Bill stopped regularly attending AA meetings stating he felt he was always asked "to speak as the co-founder of AA rather than as just another alcoholic."[39] That was understandable. After Dr. Bob's death in 1950 at the age of 71, when AA was just 15 years old, Bill was left to be the only living founder of AA. He still, however, believed that:

> *"...no individual member is ever recognized as a spokesperson for the Fellowship locally, nationally, or internationally. Each member speaks only for himself or herself."* [40]

In recent times, however, it can sometimes seem as though AA has people in charge, deciding what can be said or done at a meeting or even how to "do" AA. If you've ever been to a meeting in many of the cities in the US - and perhaps abroad, as well - you have probably seen, heard and experienced this. The "suggestions" of AA are often conveyed to new members in such a way that it is clearly understood that they will either do things the way the group does or find themselves excluded if and when they return. This hardly seems to be in line with the simple "desire to stop drinking" as "the *only* requirement for membership." (emphasis mine)

What happened to AA? How did the basic orientation toward harm reduction change? And what undermined these original principles? To understand that, we need to look at the phenomenon of the explosion of alcohol and other drug treatment beginning in the 1980s when treatment changed from a strictly inpatient, residential model to offering a variety of outpatient services. In order to accommodate this shift, treatment facilities began to use AA regularly as an adjunct to their outpatient services. Soon, AA meetings became inundated with participants who began to share their experiences of treatment and spoke in a language quite unfamiliar to AA members at the time: "child of an alcoholic;" "the disease concept;"[41] "codependency;" "therapy-speak[42]" etc. This led to some animosity from some old AA-ers who felt that treatment was an "easier, softer way" to achieve sobriety. It also led to problematic issues around mixing other drug users with alcoholics. After much discussion in the service rooms of AA, there was a decision from the General Service Office to ask drug users to refrain from speaking at AA meetings unless they were also self-professed alcoholics – and then to keep their discussions to the topic of alcohol only.[43] The reason given for this decision was to keep the singleness of purpose, which Bill W. had often mentioned as crucial to the longevity and clarity of AA, and not dilute the work of AA. This move by GSO, however, raised the threshold for acceptance into membership in AA and accelerated its move away from harm reduction.

The decision to ask drug users to remain silent became a weapon of sorts, wielded at vulnerable people. Often a drug user would come to a meeting, scared and alone, only to be admonished to "sit down" when he or she tried to speak (in the interest of full disclosure, I allowed this to happen in a meeting where I was the secretary and, therefore, in charge. I am deeply regretful and ashamed that I allowed this to occur as the injured parties left embarrassed and in tears). At times, so-called AA traditionalists even interrupted the shares of self-professed drug users. It became a tragically difficult time as many new members began to see themselves as equally alcoholic and other drug addicted and were not sure where to turn or what to do. In most treatment centers, patients were encouraged to introduce themselves as either an alcoholic in AA or an addict in Narcotics Anonymous[44] (soon, many in AA felt an uncomfortable schism growing in its ranks from the visible differences between these "treatment babies" and those who used only AA to achieve their sobriety or abstinence).

Bill Wilson may have foreseen these kinds of problems and more when he testified at the first hearing of the Special Sub-Committee on Alcoholism and Narcotics, held in Washington, DC, on July 30, 1969. In his talk, when asked directly by the committee if AA should be used as a model for treatment and integrated into a treatment modality, he surprised everyone by responding "no" (Bill had once dreamed of AA treatment centers all over the world until Dr. Bob talked him out of it). Perhaps he did foresee the challenges of integrating multiple problems into AA's singleness of purpose and dealing with the concerns of people attending AA who did not have a desire to stop drinking.

I hope this chapter has helped to shed a little bit of light on how and why AA and harm reduction became separated (for more, please see Ernie Kurtz's *Not-God*, the AA history books, *Dr. Bob and the Good Oldtimers* and *Pass it On* or other historical materials available through the General Services Organization. Go to www.aa.org for more information).

Bottom line, AA is not what it used to be and some of that, it seems, is what Bill Wilson - and no doubt Dr. Bob - was hoping for: that is more inclusion of all persons: women, people of color, non-English speakers and a diverse group of many others. The not-so-great part lies in the apparent shift to dogma, seemingly forgetting Bill's own words about the necessity of change and *how* AA works: Honesty, Openmindedness, and Willingness[45] - the "essentials of recovery."[46] It seems it's the "O" that has really been forgotten. Or perhaps it's simply the very nature of AA's upside-down hierarchy, which, as positive as it is, can also be what allows strong personalities to take over a meeting – either for their own egotistical needs or simply because they are such "'true believers" that they believe they have found *the only way* to recover. Either way, many folks say they feel left out, abused and re-traumatized, pressured to make changes before they're ready, or even that they are given dangerous information, all with good intentions.

And sometimes, like me, they simply leave with an aching heart and great sadness that many groups who call themselves meetings of Alcoholics Anonymous, which I was taught to love deeply enough to challenge, have become something that many of us believe Bill Wilson and Dr. Bob wouldn't agree with or recognize today.

DAN BIGG

HARM REDUCTION OLDTIMER

I came to harm reduction because I had a personal dissonance between what was being done in addiction treatment and what we knew should be done. Between a family experience with addiction and what happened in the 1980s with the outbreak of HIV infections and AIDS, my dissonance was encouraged. I was in graduate school at the time. HIV came and with it came a motivation to do things differently in addiction treatment and HIV prevention. I got involved with the HIV/AIDS prevention movement from the very beginning, and the end result was a chance - an opening - to do things differently.

With a number of other individuals, I started a support group called HIVIES – HIV Information, Education, and Support - in the late 1980's. Perry Tilleraas (Editor's Note: author, *Circle of Hope: Our Stories of AIDS, Addiction, and Recovery*; HarperCollins, 1990) in Minneapolis was doing something parallel at the time, which they called the Minnesota Recovery Alliance, or MRA. At MRA, they were dealing with traditional recovery issues *and* HIV transmission through male-to-male sex: in other words gay-friendly recovery issues. Unheard of at that time! By the way, Perry also wrote a little book in the Hazelden-published series of daily meditations for people in recovery called *Daily Meditations for All of Us Living with AIDS.* He also wrote a book for HIVIES about self-support as most of the people in HIVIES were involved, or had been, in 12-

Step recovery groups. Almost all of them also had very negative reactions to those groups.

Basically, HIVIES folks said that when they brought up issues of sexuality in AA, members told them that these were "outside issues." [Editor's note: according to AA traditions, members agree to talk about subjects only as they relate to their alcoholism. This is because AA tradition states that "AA has no opinion on outside issues" so that it will not be drawn into controversy. See the AA book *Twelve Steps and Twelve Traditions* for more.] Their sexuality brought up medical issues and those were outside issues - and AA in 1984, '85 and '86 couldn't see a connection between alcohol and HIV or AIDS. Every week we in HIVIES gathered; it was a powerful experience. I think gathering and sharing like we were doing in HIVIES is also the secret to one's finding success in 12-Step groups, too, as long as they're not punitive, manipulative or controlling. The idea of getting together with like-minded people is incredibly powerful, and this is true whether the issue is alcoholism or living well with HIV: it's that you're gathered with another warm body and they understand you in ways that most others do not, and you can talk about issues that are generally cloaked in shame and pathology. In HIVIES, we didn't discriminate, which meant anyone was free to come and share anything about themselves that they felt was important. No one would tell them "that's not related to your recovery" because we had learned that everything in our lives was related to recovery. Unfortunately this wasn't the case in AA although some specialty subgroup 12-Step meetings did begin to occur, such as meetings only for women or only for men or only for gay people.

The HIVIES groups, in general, produced a lot of friendships. The work gave meaning to my life, academically and career-wise. When I first went from the addiction world into the HIV treatment world, I attended all the HIV/AIDS conferences for which I was allowed time off. I think it was in 1985 at a conference on AIDS: I'm sitting there, trying to see this connection between addiction and HIV/AIDS. I wasn't used to feeling professionally out-of-place, but there were just amazingly few addiction colleagues in the HIV/AIDS world at that time. The speakers were talking about PCP, and I was struggling to piece it together - what did PCP, the drug, have to do with AIDS? Finally I embarrassingly asked the man next to me, "Why do they keep talking about angel dust?" [Editor's note: angel dust is another name for PCP or phencyclidine, a powerful hallucinogenic drug.] He looked at me like I was insane! Finally, I pieced it together: they were talking about pneumocystis pneumonia – nicknamed "PCP" in the HIV/AIDS world! I realized I had a lot to learn! There were a lot of challenges then, but the real challenging pieces, ironically, still exist today. Overcoming the stigmatization of the disease of HIV and AIDS took much longer than anyone thought it would but, eventually, it happened. There was an incredible amount of acceptance that took place a couple of decades ago with AIDS; sadly, I can't say the same has been true with drug issues.

It is more than a little distressing that this same level of acceptance around drug issues has still not happened. In the face of death, you would think many more people would be talking about this issue, too. I started working for the Illinois Alcohol and Drug Dependency Outpatient AIDS Project with Bella Celan, a wonderful lady. I was 26 years old and Bella was a refuge from Nazi Germany, and she moved up here due to a friendship she had developed with a professor at Northwestern University [Editor's note: Evanston, IL]. It was a wonderful time. Bella and I were doing this work together, and one of the things I wanted to do was a survey of methadone treatment programs to see how people had dealt with the HIV pandemic. My caseload at the AIDS project was showing more and more people infected with HIV. This was in 1985, and we had a research project with Emory University in Atlanta that said on intake we would ask if people were interested in having their blood tested for AIDS. Nearly everyone was interested and so got tested. Six weeks after intake, the lab slip would come back with the results: HTL-3 antibody positive or negative, so we learned about people's HIV status right at the starting point, when it first impacted people. We also began to incorporate their status into their methadone treatment plans.

I remember this Puerto Rican man saying to me, "How can this be? I've never had sex with a man at all." I had to say I didn't know – because we didn't know back then that people could and were contracting HIV from drug use and not only gay sex - and then later, of course, we found out that his injection practices very clearly put him in line with being at risk for contracting HIV. We were just on the cusp of awareness of HIV. This combination of HIV treatment with addiction treatment became a sort of sad reprieve in the storm of punishment and incarceration and repression, of brutal and ineffective drug treatment; the wave of calm was, ironically,

HIV. All of a sudden, people were taking a step back to consider whether they were willing to have any compassion – for either HIV suffers or drug users - and redefine their professional roles in terms of whether they had any empathy for these clients. It was a fascinating and powerful time in drug treatment.

After leaving the position at the AIDS project, I found an internship, which was required for my counseling education (I had recently begun my studies in drug and alcohol counseling towards certification). I went to Cook County Hospital [Editor's note: Chicago, IL] with a goal of learning how to combine my work experiences in psychology, HIV and drug use into something useful for the patients there. HIV, mental health challenges, and drug use were certainly issues that existed in big ways in Chicago's Cook County Hospital, so I felt confident that this internship would be enlightening, to see how Cook County was dealing with them. However, I found out very quickly that just because those issues existed, it didn't mean that hospital workers were dealing with them. I saw that there was very little chance of combining these important patient issues for a host of reasons, one of which was that the man in charge of the drug treatment portion of the hospital was going around acting like a preacher, coming in with flowing robes to proselytize the masses! The typical outside aversion to addiction treatment is still the quasi-religious nature of much of it and, after seeing him, I could certainly see why.

So, after working in various aspects of addiction treatment – inpatient, outpatient, substitution and drug-free - since 1980, I just never felt that we were treating patients the way we would like to be treated if we were patients. These were all difficult situations for me. It seemed as though treating people with respect was seen as less-than-helpful, or even in conflict with these treatment programs. We have learned in recent years, because of Miller [Editor's note: William R. Miller, co-author, *Motivational Interviewing*] and others, that these confrontational methods are just bullshit. Even with William L. White [Editor's note: a well-known speaker, author and prominent historian on treatment and recovery who lives in the Chicago area; author, *Slaying the Dragon: A History of Addiction Treatment and Recovery in America*] living here in our neighborhood in Chicago, people still think that harm reduction is for people who are too pathetic to change.

We know what works, what actually helps people make changes in their lives but instead treatment providers act like police, not trusted professionals. The question is, "Is there room in our treatment programs for a cost-effective, humane treatment program that is effective without any of the harassment that is such a part of the current system?" We've shown that a harm reduction program can be both cost-effective and easily integrated into traditional treatment, yet we still aren't able to even say the words "harm reduction" and obtain Federal funding. In the UK, providers are free to prescribe heroin, but very few do probably due to a fear of harassment. Here in the States, we don't even have that option available to doctors, even if doctors felt it was medically necessary.

It was only through the combination of HIV and drug use that I became motivated to advocate for change in drug treatment and prevention. There were only about a dozen of us - through HIVIES again - that were interested in some combination treatment, with Perry Tilleraas as the catalyst. Most of us were there for support-type issues: we were there to get support and to give support. We were amazed to think that this idea for treatment that we had "hatched" in HIVIES could really be something that could actually come into practice; we were all just talking about this over coffee! A lot of people were not satisfied with just this idea of support though. One analogy was that "people are falling off the cliff so what are you going to do?" Someone said, "Why don't we put up a fence to keep people from falling?" The end result was to ask if a group like HIVIES was necessary for people to survive. We decided to meet to talk about it. There was a restaurant in Chicago called Ann Sathers and its owner, Tom Tunney, was very generous, giving us and so many people space. So Tom said, "As long as you guys need it, I'm happy to provide sweet rolls and coffee and give you this room."

At that first meeting, it was magic: we were a no-nonsense group and a magical combination of people. Again everyone was touched, in one way or another, by either drugs or HIV, or both. There were people in that room that night who were intellectually gifted and there were those who were emotional sayers of the times. This was the first time we had people from both drugs *and* HIV together, and it was the first time that we had people asking if such a group was necessary. Actually somewhere during the process, I called the folks in Minneapolis (MRA) [Editor's Note: MRA is Minnesota Recovery Alliance] and asked what they would think about our using the name *Chicago Recovery Alliance*, and they said they'd be really honored by it; they were thrilled. And so, CRA was born, as was the first support group in Chicago for people with drug and HIV problems.

As to the question of whether a group like this was needed, we all said, "Yes, absolutely!" We agreed that our one unifying belief was that the group had to be action-related - it couldn't be just another meeting. The power of this positive change was equalized; it was respectful and allowed people to define for themselves what was a positive change. Really, there was no alternative to this meeting at the time. Many people today think that it is their ministrations that are curing people, despite all the evidence to the contrary. This alternative, CRA, put the idea of recovery in each *person's* lap: recovery became personal. There is something so sane about that. But it required something that is both the crux and the challenge in addiction treatment today: it requires that we hear people. And we need to not get in their way. We also began to see that the best guide to getting people interested in some kind of recovery was to present as many options for recovery as possible. We began to see that as professionals, that's our job: remove obstacles so people can recover themselves. That is such a huge thing. George Vaillant, who wrote *The Natural History of Alcoholism*, should be in this discussion. He said effective treatment isn't the curative efforts of anyone other than the clients themselves. Those are the results of his longitudinal studies.[47] And I've certainly seen this to be true in my professional work.

So, for me harm reduction is the practice of providing as many options for positive change as one can. In our case, it is about assisting the reduction of drug-related harm, but it doesn't have to be. Harm reduction can be anything in any field that reduces harm to the individual or society. For example, many people are killed each year in the US due to automobile accidents. Yet we don't outlaw cars. Instead, we opt for laws and training to help people remember to wear seat belts, shoulder restraints, and to simply drive defensively. That's harm reduction, both for the individual and for society at large. In addiction treatment, we have the ability to help people reduce the harm to their lives from their behavior and gain access to that assistance by working collaboratively toward any positive end. Both the topic and the intensity of the treatment must be determined *entirely* by the person seeking help. Also, we need to be providing this engagement through a reflective feedback system, an alliance to facilitate any positive change as defined by the people themselves.

Bill Miller might call this a "bouquet of options." What I'd say is that the *quantity* of those options is also important. To me, this idea of the options we give to clients is rather like setting out selections on a banquet table: we need to think of all the people who are coming to eat, not just the vegetarians or such. So, someone may want a little taste of the mashed potatoes, and someone else may want a whole plate of it, and someone else wants none at all. We need to offer something for everyone, for all different tastes. You can also make multiple trips to the banquet table, so treatment needs to be open-ended with the understanding that it's also okay to throw out the whole plate and start fresh. What's really important is that the clients, like the buffet eaters, make their own selections. So many programs are basically serving up food on your plate for you, rather than just guiding you to the table and showing you the options. That *guiding* toward any positive change is harm reduction, and that's what real treatment – and treatment professionals - should be doing.

Dan Bigg is the Director of Chicago Recovery Alliance (CRA), a no-threshold harm reduction information and needle exchange organization in Chicago, IL. See www.anypositivechange.org for more information and to reach Dan.

PATT DENNING

HARM REDUCTION OLDTIMER

When I look back on it, I've come to realize that I actually took a direct route to harm reduction, going back to 1972. However to others, it probably seems like I began in harm reduction closer to 1989 as that was when the term began to be used here in the States and I became publicly active in the movement.

In 1972, I was working in a maximum-security juvenile center as a science Special Education teacher in St. Louis, Missouri. It didn't take me long to realize, though, that these kids couldn't read worth a darn and they weren't at all interested in chemistry and the like! So if I was going to survive, I was going to have to do something they were more interested in. It wasn't too hard for me to figure this out as I was only 21 at the time and figured that since they weren't that much younger than I, we were probably all interested in the same kinds of things: sex, drugs, and rock and roll! So, I developed a life-skills curriculum about sex and drugs and we listened to rock and roll during class. As there weren't many materials for drug education, I brought in the PDR [Editor's note: the *Physician's Desk Reference*, which lists information on all the medications available by prescription in the US, updated annually]. At this time in St. Louis, there weren't any real street drugs, which meant that these kids were going into their mom and dad's medicine cabinets and taking their prescriptions.

The PDR allowed me to show them pictures of prescriptions, and I would ask them to point to the drugs they were taking, then

I would read them the description of that pill. Sometimes it was really hysterical. I would ask them, "So how many of these did you take?" And the kid would say, "Oh, I took a handful of these," pointing. And I'd ask, "So what happened?" And sometimes they would say, "Oh, I just shit my pants!" Then I would look up the medication and we'd discover that it was indeed a stool softener! So we had a lot of fun while getting the message across to these kids that not everything in the medicine cabinet can get you high; some of it can make you sick. Even when there was something that could kill them, I needed to make a bit of a joke about it. These were tough kids after all; so threatening them with the this-can-kill-you message wouldn't work. I really think this was my first experience on the harm reduction track.

    I didn't do much with that first experience but, soon after, I came to San Francisco in 1978 as the director of a psychiatric residential program. Harm reduction sort of cropped up there unconsciously for me when we were trying to decide about the meaning of rules in a milieu. What we decided was that, other than for California State licensing requirements, we shouldn't make any rules that adult people wouldn't be likely to make for themselves (mind you, you couldn't do this now). So we didn't have any rule against sex in the house, but we did talk to people about the fact that if you have special relationships in the house everyone really does know and has feelings about it, so it's probably better not to be secretive about it as most adults probably wouldn't be secretive about their sex lives. And we didn't have any rule against drinking. We didn't even need to articulate rules about illegal drug use since, at that time, there was very little illegal drug use by folks with schizophrenia. This is totally different now, of course. But the folks at our program would simply abuse alcohol sometimes, so the rule that we made was that you couldn't go to your bedroom and drink – that the adult way of drinking is to be sociable, in public. Therefore if you're going to be drinking - and it would be nice to also share though you didn't have to - you should do it in the social areas of the milieu. One of the great things about this approach is that staff always knew what was going on. This way, if we observed that someone who typically didn't drink much was sitting in the TV room with a six-pack between their legs, we'd know to check in with them to see what was going on. Then we got to talk to the person. Sadly, this little experiment ended when a particular contract person came in for an inspection of the facility and hit the roof when she heard about our way of dealing with patients drinking! But this went on for a few years before we were forced to stop.

Then in 1983, I went to an outpatient program in the Castro [Editor's note: a famous mainly gay district of San Francisco], which was ground-zero for the HIV epidemic, and two things really happened there: 1) for the first time, I was working with a multi-disciplinary team that included a lot of public health doctors and nurses, lots of whom had been in the Peace Corps, and 2) we were seeing numerous seriously ill people who couldn't physically get to treatment that was often located quite a distance from our clinic.

These public health nurses and doctors who had been in the Peace Corps were much more welcoming and flexible with people, and they did a lot more outreach and engagement. For instance, if somebody didn't want to come into the clinic, these doctors and nurses might go do a home visit. They would go talk to the person and kind of cajole them or offer them incentives of some kind like a meal or something. We clinicians thought this was just *so* unprofessional. But the public health folks looked at us as if we were idiots. They would say to us, "You mean your client didn't show up - and you didn't go and find them?" And so I got this taste of "gee, maybe there's another way of doing this that really has to do with *engagement*." I began to understand that what we needed to do was get off our butts and engage folks in treatment, not just sit and wait for them to 'be ready." It was during this period, I believe it was 1989, that I heard about this group called the Harm Reduction Coalition and read a little bit about needle exchange. We'll get back to that.

The second thing that happened to me while I was the director of this program in the Castro was that a lot of the guys coming in for services had substance abuse problems - not just mental health problems. Some of them had been having trouble for a while in their lives, and others had clearly developed these problems as a result of all the stress from the epidemic: watching friends die. At that time, we had a policy that stated if you had a substance abuse problem, you had to go to treatment; you couldn't just come in for mental health services. So we were pretty much just willy-nilly referring people to substance abuse treatment, and two things were happening: 1) they wouldn't go to treatment or would drop out immediately or 2) they were so sick they couldn't go. Understand, our clients would come into our clinic and would have their primary care physician and their therapist right there. But they couldn't get across town [Editor's note: in San Francisco, substance abuse services were located across town, not in the same building as mental health and medical services]. They were so sick and they were dying so fast that they just couldn't physically get there. So we quietly changed our approach, starting with the sickest ones - and maybe the people who were most willing - and instead of enforcing the "you must go to treatment" rule, we just didn't send them to substance abuse treatment. Instead, we simply started talking to them about their drug use at the clinic. Well, I should say that *I* started talking to them. Most of the other staff, who were old-time licensed community mental health folks, didn't mind if *I* talked to these substance abusers, but *they* weren't going to do it. So I did. I just started talking to people about their drug use. And interesting things began to happen.

I guess I've always had a different perspective on drug use due to my interest in pharmacology - it's my big love – ever since I was a kid reading my father's medical books (he was an MD) –and spending time memorizing the PDR. I thought I wanted to be a doctor, too, so I guess I had this type of medicalized background, and substance abuse fit into that construct for me – it was about pharmacology. Of course I'd also done my own experimenting with drugs and plenty of booze, growing up in the Midwest, driving around in high school with cases of beer in the car (I look back on it now and wonder what were we thinking? Gratefully, most of us survived it). So I had my own knowledge about substance abuse and my own ideas about substance use such as: you can indeed use chemicals and not get into trouble with it just as I had done! I also knew that you could use drugs and have a lot of fun. I just didn't see people with knock-down, drag-out addictions around me. The people coming into our Castro clinic were pretty much folks with long-standing alcohol addictions but, in terms of other drugs, those other drugs would have been all new to our folks. Our folks might have partied here and there but now, all of a sudden, they were experiencing some pretty severe abuse or addiction problems. These were pretty uncomplicated folks, not engaging in any behaviors that would lead you to mistrust them either. I'd say they were "stress users." The worst trouble they got into was probably driving while pretty drunk and stoned - and that wasn't good. So my observations of alcohol and other drug use and problems changed and, at the same time, I wanted to check out these drug treatment programs where I was sending people because I wanted to figure out why folks didn't want to go: I knew clinically that they really needed help and they weren't getting it.

My assumption was that these programs were probably homophobic as our clients were from the Castro (not to mention oftentimes suffering with HIV/AIDS). So I went to visit Walden House, Haight-Ashbury Free Clinics, Henry Ohlhoff House, and a couple of other San Francisco outpatient clinics, and the first thing I thought was how weird it was that they let me sit in on their groups; I was blown away by that. And then I saw what was going on, and I was *appalled* at the way these programs treated people. They were accusatory and confrontational. If a person started talking too much about what was going on in their life and how they were feeling, the group leader basically told them to shut up and listen. People were being told that they were "just making excuses" for their chemical use. So there was this high level of confrontation and what I saw as disrespect, and then there was this whole general atmosphere of "you addicts are ABC and D." There was this homogenization, this lack of belief in the individualization of people in these treatment programs.

Furthermore, as I talked to them, the staff had pretty much all come through the program where they were working. So that fed this idea that "if it worked for me, it will work for you if you just try hard enough." There was also a lot of "the Big Book says..." and I'd ask, "What's the Big Book?" When I did get a Big Book, the main book of AA, it was my next level of being appalled.

While reading the Big Book, I remember thinking, "Who is this arrogant bastard who wrote this thing?" Then I tried to put a cultural perspective on the book: written in the 1930s by a white, upper-middle class man who thought he knew better than anybody, but there was still this feeling of "we alcoholics are different than you; we're special, we're different, we're screwed up, nobody can help us, and nobody can understand us." The religious stuff also made me go nuts. This was all in the late 1980s and early 1990s. I came away from these experiences saying, "No wonder people won't go to these places; I wouldn't go either!" I knew I wouldn't want to be treated that way. But people said that I really needed to go to AA meetings because that was where things really happened.

So, I started attending AA meetings. I probably went to 50 different ones. And at this point I think we had started to use the term dual-diagnosis, but we certainly knew that at the clinic we were getting more and more people who had serious mental illnesses along with substance problems: they weren't your regular, run-of-the-mill alcoholics. And they were reporting that they felt weird at these AA meetings. So part of me wanted to see what these meetings were about, and part of me wanted to find meetings that our folks might be able to attend and feel comfortable to get some additional support. I did find some that were okay but many still made me squirm. I didn't like the slogans and especially the no cross-talking rule [Editor's note: "cross-talk" is defined in AA as talking to one another in a meeting. In AA, people are asked not to do this; instead, members are to speak only after the other member is finished and then not to respond directly to that member's monologue]; one person would be sobbing about something and the next person would describe something they had read in the Big Book, not acknowledging this person's pain and experience at all. And I just thought, as a person and as a therapist, that this was just a horrible way to treat a person! I will say, though, that I had a less intensely negative experience at meetings than at the treatment programs. I was really enraged at these programs: people at those meetings were rude and sarcastic, especially to new people. I couldn't see where any "treatment" was happening at any of them. It was awful. On the positive side, though, I was really beginning to understand the resistance of my clients to going to treatment, and I vowed I would never send them to these programs again. But that left me with "so *now* what do I do with these folks?"

And what I did was begin to take these folks with substance abuse problems and mental health problems and just work with them. I just started *talking* to folks, doing therapy. It helped some people and didn't help other people, honestly. I learned a lot about what an addictive or abuse cycle is like for people. I still wasn't really *doing* anything. It was about 1989 or 1990 when I heard about the Harm Reduction Coalition [HRC] and went to a meeting that was all about needle exchange and HIV prevention (which I was really involved with) and I discovered how much I liked these folks – they made sense! So I got involved with HRC and went to some of their trainings, and then I got word from somebody that this woman, Edith Springer [Editor's note: Edith Springer, ACSW, is a harm reduction old-timer in New York City), was coming to the General [Editor's note: the nickname for San Francisco General

Hospital, the county hospital]. I went to hear her talk and that was it for me! I was just so excited and so vibrating! Edith mentioned many people's names which I wrote down, and I started looking them up in the library, and then this entire intellectual landscape opened up for me: Alan Marlatt, Bill Miller, Reid Hester, people in the UK. I began reading all these people's works and realized that here were these mostly psychologists who have been actually studying substance abuse, and they have all these theories and ideas, which are almost all research-based, and I felt both really excited and really ripped off from all my education. There was this whole other way of thinking out there that was much more intellectual, which was important to me, that made more sense and was more humane. So I just started incorporating these things into what I was doing with my clients at the clinic and that seemed to make a huge difference: people seemed to stay in treatment longer, they seemed to get better, and they were really honest about their lives. Then I quit my job with San Francisco in 1993 and went into fulltime private practice.

I had maintained a small private practice focusing on mental health, and now I began accepting people with substance abuse problems as well. I think I began to gain a reputation for doing that [Editor's note: at this time it was still fairly unusual for substance abuse and any mental illness diagnosis to be treated concurrently]. At some point, perhaps 1996, I named my business Addiction Treatment Alternatives (ATA), came up with the website and logo and started offering trainings in harm reduction and ATA. I just kept doing more studying and working and then began doing some trainings for HRC on pharmacology. They were suspicious of me as I was a psychologist, but they appreciated that I knew a lot about drugs, so this was the way I began to work with them. I got more and more involved with them: read everything and attended all their trainings. Then in 1996 or so, I ended up on a panel with Alan Marlatt at the Harm Reduction Conference in Oakland (CA). I just loved him! I had read all his writings, of course, and he encouraged me to write about what I was doing stating that no one was really doing on-going work with this population of dually-diagnosed people. Alan became my mentor, invited me up to the University of Washington to talk to his post-doctoral students and opened up his library to me. I took everything I could and read and read. And then, with Alan's pushing, I started writing this book on what I began to term "harm reduction psychotherapy."

The book came out in 2000 after some glitches, and this was when I met Jeannie Little. We both had backgrounds in community public health, and we decided to start a non-profit for drug and alcohol treatment and dual diagnosis that would be a treatment and training center and do research on harm reduction psychotherapy. We become incorporated, began to raise funds, and hit many hurdles. We became a State-certified program, even though the requirements of the State of California were that the goal of all AOD (alcohol and other drugs) programs be abstinence. We were fully prepared to call in the Drug Policy Alliance to sue the State if they didn't allow us licensure based solely on our clients' abstinence status. We came up with wording on which we could all agree and become the first State-certified harm reduction treatment program – and perhaps the first in the United States! And here we still are, growing and continuing to find ways to bring harm reduction psychotherapy to as many clinicians and laypersons as possible!

For me, the real definition of harm reduction treatment or therapy is about using Motivational Interviewing [Editor's note: a way of being with people that involves collaboration, evoking reasons to change from the client and working towards a client's autonomy. See *Motivational Interviewing* by William Miller and Stephen Rollnick, Guilford Press, 2002, for more] as the basis for establishing a relationship with a person to help them make decisions about what they might want to do about their substance use and/or mental health. And then to use other evidence-based practices such as cognitive-behavioral therapy and include enormous work with trauma, all within a psychodynamic construct of working with the unconscious, including resistance, and transference and countertransference.

The goal is harm *reduction* – to reduce drug and alcohol- related harms and if that means helping a person, motivating a person to realize that abstinence might be their best choice, or perhaps some kind of moderation, then we're actively involved with helping people to reduce harm in those ways, while being respectful of whatever they ultimately decide to do. And, no matter what you decide, you can still come to treatment. All we ask is that you be willing to come and talk – about anything. Our agenda is certainly to reduce alcohol and other drug-related harm, at least to the community, but hopefully to the individual as well. We are always honest and upfront about this agenda. We challenge our clients to explore their ambivalence and sometimes directly intervene. I suggested recently to a husband that he install a Breathalyzer in the car because his wife was drinking and driving with their kids in the car. We don't shy away from talking to people about some really dangerous behaviors – like drinking and driving - and really getting on them to make some changes. I think this is one of the biggest misconceptions about harm reduction psychotherapy – this mistaken idea that treatment is just haphazard, that we don't encourage clients to make healthy and helpful changes in their lives. This simply isn't true. Why would we want people to continue to harm themselves or their loved ones? It's just that, bottom line, we need to remember that people always have the right to make whatever decisions they want – for better or worse. And that's true harm reduction.

Patt Denning is the Clinical Director of the Harm Reduction Therapy Centers in San Francisco and Oakland, CA. For more information, and to contact Patt, go to www.harmreductiontherapy.org.

TOM HORVATH
HARM REDUCTION OLDTIMER

I've been in the harm reduction world from my first class in graduate school. I was exposed to one class on alcoholism where the 12-Step model was advocated and it just didn't make any sense to me. First of all, it was a religious model. I don't object to people having religious beliefs that would influence recovery and in fact I encourage that, but I didn't think that it should be the only approach. Also, the notion that AA was the only thing that seemed to be available to drug users seeking change – well, that *really* didn't make any sense to me. Finally, in my post-doc placement, I did a four-week rotation in an in-patient alcoholism program and that really cemented my belief in harm reduction practices over a disease or religious model.

My post-doc rotation was at the Naval Hospital in Bethesda, Maryland. I don't remember a lot of specifics anymore, but I do remember that I was impressed with some of the group therapy that was facilitated by some outside mental health consultants. I recall this one female consultant especially: I was under the impression that she was working on some powerful issues with our clients, but then I began to see how the treatment program had become stereotypical treatment, not individual. After I sat in on a third group where a guy did a sort of discharge planning which sounded so repetitive, I realized that these groups weren't individualized to the patient. These are two of my earliest experiences in addiction treatment where I can recall thinking we need to be doing something different.

When I started my private practice in San Diego, California in June 1984, by coincidence I had a handful of patients in the first six months who came in with presenting problems of a mental health nature but who also had addiction problems. When I started to address both of these issues with them, I discovered that all of them were not at all interested in attending 12-Step. About that time I was contacted by a group out of Orange County (California) that was offering to do some training to help people become affiliates of their program. I got involved with them starting in January of 1985. I had announced a specialization in addiction as I rapidly geared myself up. At the time there weren't a lot of training opportunities for psychologists for continuing education - the theory was that you basically just had to read and keep up on topics on your own. As I got involved with addiction, I gradually came to appreciate the scientific literature more and more. In fact, my overall perspective now is based on the clear recognition that telling people what to do is wasted breath, and that came from studying the scientific papers on what was working in addiction treatment. What these studies were saying was, essentially, if the consequences of addictive behavior hadn't convinced folks to change their behavior, then there's nothing *I'm* going to say that's going to make a difference!

So I'd say I have an overall harm reduction approach. I think that to do that consistently means that you have a policy that says, "Regardless of your substance or your level of problems, you choose whether to abstain, moderate, or just cut back." And you can choose to abstain on one substance and not do anything about another substance - it's entirely up to the client. So it's sort of a 'harm reduction/Motivational Interviewing with skills-building approach' that recognizes that almost everybody is "dually-diagnosed" in the sense of having multiple issues. Also, even if you can't make headway immediately on the addiction issue, you can probably make headway with some of the other issues and then come back around and help the addiction issue. It's all connected anyway.

In terms of ideas helping me "come" to harm reduction, there's probably no one more important than Stanton Peele. Certainly Bill Miller and Alan Marlatt are very important. Also Aaron Beck who provided the framework for helping people think accurately, but also the whole Existential Movement: the recognition that this is your life and you get to choose how to use it; you use it or lose it. I know Beck's idea was when somebody presents an automatic statement like, "I'm a failure" or "I'm stupid," as a clinician, you don't automatically go in and judge that thought to be wrong or bad; first you analyze it in an open-minded way. You need to ask, "What is the evidence?" and it turns out, as far as I'm concerned, that *every* thought has some element of truth in it, even if it's perhaps distorted or wrong. I take the same approach with addictive behavior.

I don't automatically assume that so-called addictive behavior is wrong or bad. Let me give you an example: you're dying from cancer and your physician won't prescribe morphine out of fear that you'll become physically dependent. The notion of addiction is meaningless in that context because there are benefits to taking the morphine. Will you become physically dependent? Sure! But who cares? You're dying.

I take an open-minded approach with people. In fact I would have to say one of my proudest moments in my professional life was when I was working with a heroin addict who assumed that I was a recovered heroin addict - and actually I'm not recovering in any traditional sense of that word but I really appreciated his thinking I was. Why? Because I truly believe we all have addictive behavior of some kind. I think that we are wired to be food, sex, and attention (from others) addicts, and that's what allows us to survive both individually and as a species. And, furthermore, I believe that other addictions have arisen from cultural developments, both due to psychoactive substances and to activities like gambling and shopping, and they didn't really emerge until our current culture emerged. They're *not* a part of our original wiring or our long-term evolution.

The substances and activities piggyback on to the established reward systems of food, sex and attention, or we can even say "hijack" those systems. This really makes sense to me because with severe addictions, you see people do things - they work to get their substance as if their lives depended on it - and that's what food and sex and attention are for us: our lives *do* depend on them. Starting in 1995 I got some fresh experience with this. I began using an approach to eating known as *calorie restriction*, an approach to increasing longevity that was identified nearly 100 years ago. Calorie restriction involves reducing food intake dramatically and is based on a discovery that various laboratory animals can live up to 50% longer than those who are fed a normal calorie diet. I am a fairly thin person but, in the process of doing calorie restriction, I coped with hunger on a daily basis, and I think it's really helped to inform my addiction work. When I was single, I was furiously single, so if I had an addiction in those days it was probably sex. So even though I never had any *substance* addictions, I had others. I tell people, "There's really nothing wrong with getting high." In fact, as Ron Siegel suggests, the drive to intoxication is really a fourth drive state: food, sex, fluids, and intoxication. I think that may be right. Once people get intoxicated *then* we crave to go back for more. But really the question is *how* can I get intoxicated? So I'm not opposed to *intoxication*, just getting there with substances that are damaging.

Let's look at another way people become intoxicated. I'm thinking about the use of religion. Religion is intoxicating for many people. That is part of its draw. So you can certainly become intoxicated by almost anything, depending on what it is that excites you, that brings you passion in life. And we can look at people's emotional and physiological maturity in terms of what intoxicates them. With addictions, we're just trying to move people up the ladder so that they get involved with intoxications that are less harmful to them. The harm reduction approach works on the whole spectrum of the ladder: if I were going to sit down with the Dalai Lama and he were to analyze my life, he might have as much pity on me as I do the homeless heroin user. He might think of me, "Boy, this guy doesn't have much of a life!" But if the Dalai Lama were using a harm reduction approach, he might nudge me in the direction of meditating more or being kinder to animals, whatever might lead to a rise in my consciousness and maturity. I think it's the same model in treating addictions.

I do very occasionally have clients who are interested in attending and utilizing 12-Steps. But frankly nobody shows up here looking for 12-Step since we screen potential clients by phone. So there are very few people that would call looking for 12-Step: they would simply call 12-Step itself. Occasionally we have referred people to 12-Step or back to 12-Step. If I think our program has so many choices that you'll be overwhelmed, I might suggest that you might do better in a program like 12-Step where others would just tell you what to do. And that's okay if that's what you want. So that's one issue: sometimes people decide themselves that they want to go back to 12-Step-- almost everyone who's getting treatment here was originally in 12-Step. I had one woman who called a few years ago. She said she had heard about Smart Recovery and she was thinking that maybe she should go to check out a meeting. So she called us to find out about the meetings and said she was actually pretty happy with AA. I really tried to talk her out of changing to us! I told her she was always welcome to go to the Smart Recovery meetings but if what she was doing was working, why change?

If someone asks me to summarize what Smart Recovery is, I just tell them the approach is very different from 12-Step, and if 12-Step works for you, great, but if you're looking for an alternative this might be for you. We teach *self-empowerment,* not powerlessness, as we view addiction as a complex, maladaptive behavior and not as a disease. I also tell people they could moderate or abstain - that's up to them – and that they don't need to go to meetings, even Smart Recovery meetings. Instead, they could go to groups or individual one-on-one therapy, or both: they are entirely in charge. We have a program where clients are in charge: they come in as often or as little as they like. People don't need us to change them; they can change their behavior any time it's important to them. It's not a disease, therefore, clients are in charge and if they need help deciding what is more important, or if they realize how important changing is, we can happily talk about that. Most of our time in treatment is spent on finding other intoxicants or helping clients manage moods or improving their relationships. We actually spend little time on the addiction itself and that time, if a client just reads the workbook and reads it thoroughly, well that covers the addiction piece pretty well; we work with clients on the rest of the stuff. And that's harm reduction to me.

A. Thomas Horvath ("Tom") is the President of *Practical Recovery*, a treatment program in La Jolla, CA, that does not use a 12-Step model. For more information, or to reach Tom, please go to www.practicalrecovery.com.

MARC KERN

HARM REDUCTION OLDTIMER

Harm reduction is a group of ideas, part of which I do a lot of work in: that part is Moderation Management (MM). MM was founded by Audrey Kishline[48], and the *incorrect* version states that she was attending MM when she had a deadly alcohol-related car accident. Actually, Audrey had been attending AA and had been doing so for several months before and at the time of the crash. Sadly, the reality is that this false story has even been used for abstinence-only leverage with clients at the Betty Ford Clinics and remains an urban myth in many treatment circles. I recently heard this myth retold by a client who had brought up the idea of trying something short of abstinence to the staff at Betty Ford and was told that "Audrey tried to control her drinking and see what happened to her!" They forthrightly misrepresented the details.

I was always a harm reductionist. I was an architect by degree, but I got into Quaaludes™ (Editor's note: a once very popular barbiturate, or "downer") and a lot of other drugs leading to a full-blown addiction to downers including alcohol. I figured out that there might be an opportunity to "kill two birds with one stone" so I went back to school - CSPP [Editor's note: California School of Professional Psychology] - and tried to resolve my addiction and get a PhD because I couldn't go back to architecture since I had two grand mal seizures trying to detox from Quaaludes™ right in front of 60 other architects (not a good career move!). I was really ashamed and embarrassed about that incident.

Coming to Harm Reduction Kicking & Screaming

My story of addiction and redemption, if you will, is almost the opposite of everyone else's. I went to CSPP where, ironically, they knew nothing about addiction; there were no classes that talked about it. I started to read the literature and do my dissertation on the topic - not on harm reduction but on addiction. So, I read all the classical psychoanalytical works, all the classical behavioral works, and all the classic works that had been written up to that time about addiction. I came out of CSPP a full-blown harm reductionist though I didn't have the term "harm reduction" then. You know, classic psychology is all harm reduction. It doesn't know anything else, and it was like a shock to me that the addiction people didn't legitimatize it. I mean we don't look for depression abstinence or anxiety abstinence. What sort of a concept is that? But somehow these two worlds separated and became polar opposites.

After graduation, I went out for my first job interview as a newly minted psychologist, and the interviewer said to me, "How do you conceptualize addiction?" I said, "Essentially it is an adaptation that has gone awry," and he said, "Get out of here, you're going to kill people." I was shocked. I didn't even know that I wasn't even on the right planet about abstinence – not for patients and not for myself! I had never fully quit anything. I mean I stopped my Quaaludes™ but I kept on drinking, less and less and less and less, and went through a Valium™ phase and Xanax™ phase [Editor's note: Valium™ and Xanax™ are both anti-anxiety drugs available by prescription]. I hadn't even realized the essentialness of abstinence until I went out into the "big world" and they slam-dunked me for thinking in this crazy way. So, really I only learned about abstinence after I learned about harm reduction, not the other way around. I had never even heard of AA until *after* I got my PhD, and by then I was already a harm reductionist.

How did we get into the dilemma that we're in? The society that I live in has bought this idea that everyone is an addict and they have a problem, and yet that's not been my experience. And there is mandated 12-Step attendance, but no one has apparently even thought that perhaps the person has some mental health issues going on and those must be treated more slowly. With mental health disorders, you reduce the symptomology to help someone function better; there is no concern that someone be *abstinent* from their mental health symptoms!

I hear so many stories from my clients - my harm reduction clients especially – that their families don't believe in the harm reduction treatment they're doing in therapy because I don't mandate abstinence from the get-go from them (families are rightfully scared for their loved ones but also need to understand that I can't force patients to do *anything* any more than they can). Often, we will even be heading towards abstinence, but since we didn't start there, the family will say our plan is doomed to fail. I have had many clients who stop their alcoholic drinking and become able to drink socially and, eventually, the family is able to accept their moderation as life becomes less chaotic. But for your typical addiction professional, this harm reduction or moderation concept is just impossible to reconcile with their training. I recently spoke for an agency here in Los Angeles on the topic of "alternatives to abstinence." There must have been 150 people in the room, and I could see that some of the people there were nodding their heads and saying, "Yeah," agreeing with much of what I was saying. And then there were others who seemed so tense and angry - rage was clearly building up inside them. I had no idea how to soothe them. I gave them logic; I gave them reason; and I gave them research, but it was like there was a cognitive dissonance or something that caused some in this audience to be unable to hear any of it – like flat-world believers.

I think part of this phenomenon of not understanding harm reduction is because we are asking a number of professionals to disrupt their entire paradigm of life to see another perspective in addiction treatment. Culturally, we have constructed an organization of understandings about addiction, and the traditionalists want to keep it all in place. When I did the ABC television news show "20/20" many years ago, I was one of the main speakers. I didn't get death threats, but I did get a number of other types of threats including email threats. I was honest to goodness scared after the episode aired. My wife was scared because she and my kids were on the show, too. This whole anti-harm reduction/pro-abstinence only movement is scary because this isn't just people saying, "I don't agree with you": it's *rage*, and it's irrational.

But it's not just some AA members who are irrational. I've known Audrey Kishline for many years. She was on a TV show down here in LA many years ago. I went just to accompany her this particular time and there were some SOS folks [Editor's note: Secular Organization for Sobriety] in the audience freaking out at what she was saying about moderate drinking. Absolutely freaking out because, like AA, SOS is disease-based and abstinence-based. So it's not just some 12-Steppers who feel this way.

And you know, I think for some people fighting addiction, it's like talking harm reduction undermines their fundamental paradigm. The reality is it takes an immense amount of courage to pull off stopping the use of any elixir. I can look back and think about how much courage it took me to face my own demons. To think that someone is actually out promoting something short of having to stop that elixir completely, well it *is* scary for some people to hear that I didn't really need to go through the agony that many do who choose an abstinence recovery, or that I didn't have to go through the standard methodology; it seems to minimize their efforts to do so.

The population we are serving as professionals is being torn apart and people are as well because there is no synthesis, no integration of these differing philosophies. I can't tell you how many sessions where I have done just debriefing with people from a 12-Step paradigm; just course-correcting, not really doing any therapy per se. I'm just working to help them see their behavior, and their treatment choices, in a more holistic perspective with abstinence being *included* in those choices but not mandated. Sometimes a client's life will have improved substantially, but she isn't quite abstinent yet so she'll say she feels that she isn't doing enough or not doing things "right." It's very difficult — people's lives are at stake - and sometimes the traditionalists see us as a threat to people's lives instead of appreciating that we in harm reduction are often the road to abstinence for patients. Sometimes we are also seen as a threat to the traditionalists' livelihood, and they take that very seriously. I do worry though sometimes that I should have said no to a client: "No, I won't work with you because you're drinking irresponsibly." They do occasionally get behind the wheel of a car or do something else dangerous, so I wonder should I have said, "No, I'm not going to work with you if you drink and get behind the wheel ever?" Although it sometimes concerns me, ultimately, I realize that if someone is in my office seeking some change, they have a much better chance of making healthier choices for their lives than if they do nothing at all.

Harm reduction is challenging work. Some clients are very high-functioning people but there are always some difficult calls, and sometimes I really do know in my heart-of-hearts that I would prefer it if a client was abstinent. Abstinence is easier — for me and for the client. Some people want me to cut these clients off from treatment and say, "if you are not willing to accept abstinence, you can't work with me." Well, I ask which harm is greater: their not being in treatment at all or my working with someone who refuses to comply with my professional opinion? And I honestly don't know the answer to that question. Not too long ago this woman came in who was suicidal and wanted to drink moderately. I thought she had borderline personality disorder, and I wanted her to be abstinent; her psychiatrist wanted her to be abstinent. Would she work with me if I wanted her to be abstinent? No, she said. Did she go shopping for someone else to work with? Yes. Ultimately, she stayed with me, and we finally got her into a treatment program and she stabilized. She eventually became abstinent, but I didn't sleep so well for a long time because it was a much more dangerous course to take the harm reduction approach with her. But I felt she likely would have gone out and gotten drunk and committed suicide if I had mandated abstinence, as that's what she threatened. It's a tough call; I sweat it sometimes.

You know, I've never had someone come in and say, "I want abstinence" and I've said, "Oh, let's try moderation instead!" I don't do that. It's always the other way around where, in my professional opinion, given their history and the severity of their alcohol use, they should choose abstinence. But they are not willing to do that because they want a legitimate shot at moderation. It takes a lot of steps for someone to come to terms with the fact that abstinence is the only legitimate course of treatment for them to take. Usually it takes a harm reduction approach, going through all the different strategies and techniques of harm reduction psychotherapy, to give folks some legitimate reasons to come to terms with saying, "I guess abstinence is the right course for me." You know, I've never met a person who wants abstinence other than when they "hit bottom." Virtually no one *wants* abstinence. Many people have to do it, and they come to grips with this for a variety of reasons but, usually, it's through a harm reduction approach that folks will come to that perspective. But ultimately, all ways are harm reduction – and you know what? They are all tough.

Marc Kern is in private practice in Beverly Hills, CA. He can be reached through www.habitdoc.org.

JEANNIE LITTLE
HARM REDUCTION OLDTIMER

I came to harm reduction by myself. The first half of my career was spent working in domestic violence, and my first domestic violence experience was working in a shelter. I'd say it really formed my ideas about working with people in social services and ongoing therapy. My experience after that was working in group homes and residential treatment and then working again with homeless shelters and families with children. The second half of my career started in 1991 working at the Veteran's Administration Hospital at its then inpatient dual diagnosis unit, the San Francisco VA. At the time, patients really had a difficult time getting into mental health or substance abuse treatment if they had the other disorder.

    I didn't have any background with addiction treatment, but I did have a background with extremely low threshold mental health treatment, so off I went into this fascinating dual diagnosis unit where I learned an enormous amount from various folks in psychiatry. However it was also an addiction treatment facility, and I was utterly shocked, stunned and appalled at how those patients were treated: "They are all liars; they are all in denial." That's what I heard. My most vivid memory is walking into this group that I facilitated every day: the focus group in the inpatient residential setting from 9 to 10 every morning. I often co-facilitated it with one of the nurses who had a background in some of the stricter -- rigid I would say -- abusive programs like the one the VA ran down in Menlo Park. Menlo Park was fashioned after the really rigid therapeutic communities like Synanon, and former Synanon managers ran some of their units at the time. At the Menlo Park VA, patients sometimes were forced to wear a toilet seat around their neck or scrub the bathroom floor with a toothbrush. Sometimes they were kept awake for two days or told to say "I'm sorry" a thousand times and "my character sucks" and the like. So, the nurse came out of this tradition.

One morning, I arrived at the group early. A patient had gotten there earlier than I, and he was reading a magazine. The two of us just sat there, maybe five minutes before the group (I like those pre-group moments when I just get myself settled and ready). My co-leader, the nurse, walked in, saw him reading a magazine, walked up behind him, reached over his shoulder, grabbed his magazine, threw it on the table behind him, and said, "You know better than that." That was my moment when I could just feel my heart breaking. The frustration and the rage that, God knows, he must have felt. And if he had expressed it, he would have been discharged. I mean, what's wrong with reading a magazine after all? The group hadn't even started.

I felt furious for tolerating and encouraging this kind of behavior on the part of staff. I felt anguish for the patient, and I felt embarrassment for the patient. If she had not done it in front of me, I don't think he would have been embarrassed (and I don't know if he was embarrassed. He might have just been enraged). But she did it in front of me, and so he was publicly humiliated. So that was it for me. I didn't leave immediately but I became very protective of the patients and very cautious about what I shared in rounds and team meetings about what patients had talked about. I didn't want anything that I shared to be used to stimulate any cynical evaluations about where the patients were at.

That was my nature – to not impose any sort of authoritative kind of restrictions on how people define themselves and what choices they make. It comes from having a father who answered most questions with, "Because I told you so." That didn't work for me then, and I never bought it for working with anyone else. I guess harm reduction was in my nature.

I did get myself out of there as soon as I could. I had started developing this idea I had of a drop-in center for all of the many, many patients who were ineligible or unwilling to submit to abstinence-only treatment at the VA. People who just relapsed all the time and were just not going to make it in an abstinence-only program regardless of the type of structure it practiced. So, I had been envisioning this low-threshold drop-in center, and I hate to be corny, but I often said to myself and other people, "If you build it, they will come."

I finally got myself situated at the Homeless Vets Program [Editor's note: in San Francisco, California]. A good third of the folks who came through this program, which was a 14-day stabilization unit, were homeless. A third of the homeless folks in San Francisco at that time were veterans, mostly from the Viet Nam war and, of course, the rates of substance abuse and dual diagnosis then were enormous, particularly the rates of post traumatic stress disorder or PTSD. In 1991 (when I started at the VA), PTSD had only been acknowledged by the VA for the previous ten years and, at that time, the vets who were there were between 35 and 45 years old.

I managed to get myself situated as a case manager for Health Care for Homeless Veterans (HCHV). We would see about 100 people every day. HCHV used to be at 13th and Mission, the Inner Mission. I printed up a flyer for this drop-in group, opened the doors and began. From what I can figure out, it was the first harm reduction group in the country and, indeed, they came! It took me about eight weeks to establish a culture where people didn't get in each other's faces; they didn't "pull each other's covers" [Editor's note: a phrase that means confronting each other on behaviors and statements]; they also didn't say, "hey, man, you can do it." I stopped all cheerleading and all confrontations with the words, "People make their own choices, and they are only going to change when it makes sense to them." I explained to them that it's really not that helpful for us to tell somebody what we think they can do; the fact that *we* think it's true doesn't necessarily make it true. So, I said I'd really like to have us not do this.

You know, the group still meets three times a week - now it's going on nearly fifteen years! I would remind people of this group and its non-confrontational nature and it made sense to them. It was an idea they weren't familiar with in addiction treatment; they were more familiar with the either the confrontation or the cheerleading - you know "come on, man, you can do it." This is lovely except when the person that you're talking to doesn't believe you. Then, it may make them feel bad because you think they *can* do it; they know they *can't* do it, and they wind up just feeling like crap for not being able to live up to other people's expectations.

The group met three times a week for eight weeks, and it took me eight weeks (24 sessions) to re-acculturate the group members to the idea that everybody should truly come as they were and everybody truly - for real, with absolutely no interference - gets to define their own problems. Over time and given the space, people's definitions of their problems became more complex. People don't really need to be pressured. At some level, whether its conscious or not, people know what they're doing. They're thinking about it in their minds or feeling it in their bodies. So giving them a totally non-judgmental and non-definitive space, they'll figure it out. So, the group was, and continues to be, unbelievably popular. I kept very rudimentary statistics, but 90% of people came back, which was a phenomenal return rate; 60% became regular members and about 30% were occasional drop-ins just to keep their toes in the group.

We really saw people change their lives there. The most common feedback is what George Gibbs, who took over the group in the late 90s, hears: "We love this group because we can be who we are and you can talk about whatever is on your mind." There is cross talk and intervention. Where there is intervention is when people start to get in each other's faces to tell somebody else the way it is. You have to ask someone permission to give them feedback. You have to know if they are in a space where they want to hear some feedback so if they say, "No, I don't want any feedback," you have to shut your mouth.   Anecdotally, lots of people improved. Lots of people got housed. We were saying to group members things like, "Hey, man, why don't you spend some of your money on an apartment and then go and use." A great quote from one of the members about creating this type of a space for people was, "You know the thing about this group that I just realized is that when I talk, that's when I figure out what I'm thinking. I don't know what I'm thinking until I talk in this group, and then I learn what I'm thinking."

After a year of running this group, I was talking to a friend in New York who was running a women's program at a hospital there, and she said, "Oh, you're running a harm reduction group." I said what's that, and she said, here, read this. So that's how I officially came to harm reduction – through creating a low-threshold group for people who didn't know what to do differently and who weren't doing it differently yet. I came to harm reduction totally purposely; I just didn't know it had a name.

The other thing I discovered accidentally was something about people who are dual-diagnosed, who couldn't get organized and who couldn't or wouldn't get themselves to other programs; they were not treated, homeless, tweaking on methamphetamine, sloshing their coffee, and nodding out. In one of my groups, a fellow case manager had sent a guy in who was heroin-dependent and homeless. He would come into the Center every morning and park his shopping cart in the corner and sit down. Then when we closed at five, he would leave. She suggested that he come to the group, which he did the second day, and he left his shopping cart in her office. He came into the group and he sat down. The chairs were set about a foot away from the wall, and he leaned his head on his shoulder and he fell asleep. People looked at me uncomfortably because what you do in a group typically when someone falls asleep is wake them up. If you're nice about it, you suggest they stand up or walk around to stay awake. I thought, "Well, here's the magazine again – what are you going to do?" I thought, "Well, he's going to wake up with a crick in his neck." So I collected a couple of jackets and very carefully rolled them up and walked over and lifted his head up to put the jacket pillow underneath. I made sure he wasn't going to have a crick in his neck! That's harm reduction, but it just made sense to me to do it.

I gained another lesson from people who had been to other groups. When I asked them what brought them to the harm reduction group, they always came to me with great humility stating they weren't doing the 12 Steps and so didn't feel that they belonged in 12-Step meetings. One of the things that was happening in treatment was that treatment programs were telling clients to change "people, places, and things," a common phrase used in 12-Step groups to describe how people need to change their surroundings to stay abstinent: homeless people - hungry, edgy, and tired. These folks could come to our group and be *with* their people in a safe environment where nobody was going to act out. Nobody used in the group, and nobody told anyone to change their surroundings: we showed them how their typical surroundings could be safe. I would say, "Your lives are hard out there" and that was all I ever said to bring calmness to the group. So they could really be honest with the full range of experiences and emotions in that group, without having to act them all out, which is my theory about harm reduction groups.

You've no doubt had a lot of definitions of harm reduction in this book, but the thing that I find compelling about it is that it's an approach where the counselor, the therapist, the staff - everyone - *completely* lets go of their agendas. It's for real — 100%. It's saying, "This is not my life and it's not my agenda."

Often the folks I work with don't know what they want; they've sort of lost the ability to dream or believe in themselves at all. I want the people that I'm working with to understand themselves better so they can figure out what they want and don't want. Hopefully, they get enough accurate information from me - or the right kind of space - and ask enough curious questions so they can figure out what they want. People can't really know what they think or know what they want or need unless they're in a neutral space. So the clinician's job is to work on ourselves to neutralize all of our busy-ness: the countertransference, or our own thoughts about the story that the person is telling, or the fact that we forgot to turn off the iron. We need to be aware of our sensations because they are information but neutralize them, minimize them to a sort of background buzz.

So how do I define harm reduction? Well, let me define harm reduction treatment. Harm reduction treatment aims to help a person whose attention has been drawn to a behavioral problem - for example, alcohol or other drugs or eating or gambling or whatever - to understand their relationship to that problem. If they're in my office, somebody — maybe themselves - has decided that it's problematic. We're in a clinical setting, and clients in a clinical setting have more problems than other people or they wouldn't be there. I see harm reduction treatment as being a process whereby the people in question understand their relationship to the behavior or to the substance, so they are free to make different choices than they have made before -- more mindful choices.

This process is the core of the work. There are many elements to it, including information. Harm reduction treatment workers should have impeccable information about alcohol and other drugs or behaviors and should have access to very knowledgeable psychiatric professionals. They should also have access to specialty treatments like trauma treatment because the coincidence of drug abuse and trauma is overwhelming. There are a lot of elements to harm reduction treatment because you need to be able to provide access to all kinds of specialized interventions. The core of the work is letting the client unfold safely and learn about self-care.

One of the things that I want to state rather strongly is what harm reduction is *not* because so many people are calling so many things "harm reduction." For example, the gradualists are calling their approach "harm reduction," and AA is sometimes called "harm reduction." I have a quote from AA: "The only requirement is a desire to stop drinking" and that's a threshold. That is a program-prescribed goal. AA is harm reducing, so things like this are harm reducing, but only when the program or goal prescribes *no goal* is it truly harm reduction as far as I'm concerned. So you can call these things harm *reductionistic* (including 12-Step), but the classic distinction between them and true harm reduction is that true harm reduction is agenda-free. The harm reduction umbrella is so broad that it is going to become the overarching model for thinking about addiction and behavioral problems in the future. It is the broadest model yet, philosophically and conceptually. It is also a paradigm shift in that it asks, "Whose agenda is it, anyway?" or "Whose life is it, anyway?" as the play asks.

The last thing I'll say about harm reduction is that it is integrative, rather than dichotomous, and purely client-driven. This is the paradigm shift. It is this integrative model where everything is understood to be influential and important in the creation of the problem and its solution(s). It is a three-dimensional rather than a linear model. And it is more complicated than traditional models, too. But then, these are people whose lives are very complicated and shouldn't treatment fit the lives of those we are treating?

Jeannie Little is the Executive Director of the Harm Reduction Therapy Center in San Francisco and Oakland, CA. For more information, and to reach Jeannie, please go to www.harmreductiontherapy.org.

G. ALAN MARLATT
ORIGINAL HARM REDUCTION OLDTIMER

My journey to harm reduction goes back to the controlled drinking controversy back in the early 1970s when some of us were trying to look at the stages of abstinence and treatment with alcohol dependents. Mark and Linda Sobell did this study in California, which then got published, leading to the follow-up by Mary Pendry and others who flatly accused the Sobells of scientific fraud. There were investigational hearings, and the Sobells ended up moving to Toronto, Canada, having been essentially forced out of the States at this point. I was doing similar kinds of work on alcohol studies regarding issues of loss of control and specifically whether people can have any drinks at all after developing alcohol dependence. I basically was one of the defenders of what the Sobells were trying to do. Various investigations that were done to see if, in fact, they falsified their data all pretty much exonerated them, but it sort of pulled me into the controversy. In fact, there was a big conference here at the University of Washington (this is probably around 1974 or '75) on controlled drinking - of course nobody was talking about harm reduction in those days. Things were really more at the stage of asking, "could you work with people who were already alcohol dependent to moderate their drinking?" But at the University of Washington, we started to move the alcohol controlled drinking project into college student heavy drinkers – binge-drinking kinds of problems - and then we obtained funding from NIAAA (National

Institute of Alcohol Abuse and Addiction) to look at whether we could do what we were calling *secondary prevention*. We were working with people that were already drinking but were not alcohol dependent. So, this project got us out of most of the controversy of whether this was a useful treatment for people who are alcohol dependent and switched it to looking at whether it was a reasonable approach for people with more of an alcohol abuse problem.

It really wasn't until the mid 1980s that people here in the States started talking about harm reduction, mainly once the link between injection drug use and HIV was realized. And I got really interested in the whole harm reduction movement while I was on a sabbatical in Amsterdam, learning about what they were doing in harm reduction. I had received an invitation from some Dutch researchers and went over to the Netherlands for three months in 1985. I was teaching them about relapse prevention, and they were teaching me about harm reduction. Now the tie-in there to relapse prevention was, even though it was originally developed as an abstinence-based approach to keep people on track, that we were asking what if they *did* relapse? How did you work with someone when they were in the middle of a relapse? This is a lot similar to what we're now doing in harm reduction therapy, working with people who are using again. The link was *relapse management*, borrowing a lot from harm reduction approaches. At this point, we no longer called this approach "controlled drinking" but more often "alcohol harm reduction programs."

In the 1990s, we developed a program called *BASICS: Brief Alcohol Screening and Intervention for College Students.* We did controlled trials looking at whether alcohol-related harm reduction that was presented in this BASICS program for incoming high-risk drinking freshmen would be effective compared to people in a no-treatment control group. We followed them up for four years after the intervention and published our final report in 2003 in the *American Journal of Public Health*. Since then, our program has been selected as a model alcohol prevention program for college students.

My interest in studying people with alcohol problems began due to having it all around me. A lot of people in my own family had alcohol problems while I was growing up. So when I got through graduate school in the 1960s at Indiana University where I had been taught about behavioral therapy, I asked my professor, "What about drinking behavior? That seems like a pretty high-risk behavior? Shouldn't we be doing some behavioral therapy approaches here?" I was basically told that this wasn't a very wise idea. My professor said that the addictions field is a pretty low priority academically. He said I should pick myself a real problem like snake phobia. I got totally discouraged from doing anything with drinking behaviors as a graduate student.

It wasn't until my internship at Napa State hospital [Editor's note: Napa, CA; State psychiatric hospital], where I got placed on the alcohol treatment ward as one of my rotations, that I started working clinically with many people with alcohol problems, and I really enjoyed it. Of course there was a very strict disease model focus: if people relapsed, they were kicked out of treatment. And I kept wondering, "why are we doing this if we tell patients that this is a disease and they can't control the symptoms and yet when they have a relapse, we kick them out of treatment?" This looked more like the *moral model* of approaching alcohol treatment. This started me thinking about relapse, relapse prevention and training people to deal with potential relapses ahead of time by looking at high-risk situations for people starting to drink again.

In those days, the main behavioral treatment for alcohol dependence was aversion therapy. My first government-funded study was looking at electrical aversion therapy for people with alcohol problems. We did the study when I was at the University of Wisconsin before I came here to the University of Washington in Seattle, looking at aversion therapy for patients at the Mendota State Hospital in Madison. Basically, we found that people who got aversion therapy drank significantly less and were more abstinent for the first three months after they got out of treatment. But then later, they actually showed higher relapse rates as compared to the control group that just got the regular 28-day program. That made us look more at relapse because we started to ask, "If people started to drink again, what was going on? Were they alone? Were they with others? How were they feeling?" And that moved me away from aversion therapy to cognitive-behavioral relapse prevention.

Now, I am definitely more into a biopsychosocial model than a strict disease model of addiction. The biopsychosocial model looks at several causal factors leading to addiction: biological factors that are critical for increasing the risk of developing dependence or abuse – for instance, a family history of alcohol problems-- and it also looks at behavior. For example, to all of the students in our BASICS program, we say, "You have a choice: you can make a decision not to drink or, if you want, you can take the course and learn how to moderate your drinking. But if you continue to see problems, you need to reconsider whether moderation is the best goal for you." We did find that a few students that went through the BASICS program ended up choosing to drink, but they got feedback that some of them just were not moderating their drinking very well. And that seemed to convince them to just give it up altogether. That switched me to thinking that rather than setting up programs where the goal is *fixed* for somebody – in other words, you can't come into our program unless you are committed 100% to abstinence from the start and where you're going to shut the door to a lot of people - instead let's have people make their *own* goals. When I was in Amsterdam, I saw they had all these low-threshold programs to get people started as well as abstinence-based programs (the abstinence-based programs were three-month inpatient programs that were very effective). But they had all these low-threshold programs where people could just get some idea of their risks. And that's what prompted us to move more in the direction away from the disease model and into a biopsychosocial-learning model. It just seemed more effective for more people.

What we mean by the difference between the two models is this: the classic disease model sees addiction as a progressive disease with no cure and believes that addiction is pretty much entirely biological; it's caused by genetic and biological factors that are beyond the person's control. The helplessness model and the helplessness and powerlessness concepts that are a part of that model are often not the best message for young people, we thought, if you want to get them to change their behavior. We don't underplay the role of biological risk genetic factors, but we're more into a continuum than a dichotomous model. The disease model states you either have the disease or you don't – think the Jellinek curve [Editor's note: see http://www.in.gov/judiciary/ijlap/docs/jellinek.pdf for more on the Jellinek Curve] and the whole downward spiral of "hitting bottom." We don't feel it's necessary for people to go all the way to "hitting bottom" before they can start to make some changes because we see people making changes all the time – before they "hit bottom."

Harm reduction, as a biopsychosocial model, is more of a continuum. What you're doing is looking at harmful consequences and putting them on a continuum in terms of what's the most dangerous about them and what people actually perceive to be helpful about their behavior, like drinking. Harm reduction has really opened up people's thinking more, for instance in needle exchange or methadone programs or maybe moderate alcohol consumption. These things just increase the probability that people will show up than would otherwise be the case. Here at the Addictive Behaviors Research Center, we started to do a study looking at mindfulness meditation as a way of helping people with addiction problems, and we've put it into a grant to NIDA to see if we can do a treatment trial [Editor's note: this study is now funded and under way and has achieved some positive preliminary results. Dr. Marlatt's presentation and his findings were very well received at the American Psychological Association Conference in San Francisco in 2007].

Gratefully, Patt Denning and Andrew Tatarsky and various other people are starting to offer harm reduction-based psychotherapy, especially to people with co-occurring disorders. They have really touched into a consumer need because there are few clinicians who are willing to see these folks. For example, I was working with this woman who had originally been referred to me through a call from a psychiatrist saying that he had been treating her for depression. Apparently he had seen her for a couple of months and she came in one day, stating she has this drinking problem. He said to me, "I don't know anything about this alcohol stuff, but I did tell her that I couldn't continue to see her until she got the alcohol problem under control. So I referred her to a recovery treatment center here, but I would also like you to do an evaluation over in the psychology department and then let me know what you think." So this woman comes in after she's already been to the treatment center, and I ask her how it's going and she said, "Everybody's telling me something different. I'm confused. The psychiatrist says I'm probably drinking to self-medicate my depression problems but he wouldn't help me with the alcohol thing, and I went to the alcohol treatment center, and they said it was the other way around – 'Your drinking is causing your depression.' This is not dual-diagnosis but more like 'dueling diagnostics' – who is going to be my service provider?" I asked her what *she* thought was really going on, and she said she thought they were both true to an extent. And she talked about how she was having a lot of problems with her marriage; she would get depressed and drink, and then her kids would find her when she was drunk and then she got more depressed – like a vicious circle. I asked her if she thought she could stop drinking as the treatment center wanted her to do and she said, "No I can't do that yet – I'm not ready. Alcohol is the only thing I can rely on. But I don't know what to do - the treatment center won't see me and the psychiatrist won't see me." So I said, "Well, *I'll* see you because we can work on both of these problems and see how they work together." She was so happy. After several months of harm reduction therapy, she ended up stopping drinking altogether and has been sober for the last eight months. And there are so many people like this out there. I think the estimates are that 80% of the people with drinking problems are not getting any help because they don't want it or maybe they don't even know it's available. If they knew that they could go somewhere and start to get some help, even if their goal was that they are not ready to stop yet –or maybe not ever – they would do something. And a lot of times, once they get going on their goal, they realize they *can* make changes, including stopping. And I think that's what will open the door for many people and just get them going - especially with folks with affective disorders that are linked to drinking and possible other drug use. And these are the folks that we really need to reach because we aren't – back to our data that show that. Bottom line, harm reduction says, "don't take a person's main coping strategies away until you have others in place." And that just seems like simple common sense to me - and the way to do real treatment.

G. Alan Marlatt is Professor of Psychology and Director of the Addictive Behaviors Research Center, University of Washington, Seattle. He is currently studying the use of meditation on relapse and can be reached at marlatt@u.washington.edu.

WILLIAM (BILL) MILLER
HARM REDUCTION OLDTIMER

First of all, I wondered about this introduction calling me a "harm reductionist," not because I am opposed to harm reduction principles, but rather because I am opposed to labels – of any kind. Generally, I don't like labels - in part because they sort of imply that you are nothing but that label. Harm reduction is one interesting issue that touches on a lot that I do, but the minute you get classified as an "-ist," that's all you are, so I resist a label like "harm reductionist." It's just too confining for me.

Initially, I got interested in alcoholism by working on an inpatient unit that had pretty severely ill folks in it – we were looking at severe alcohol dependence – and I knew nothing about alcoholism at all before that internship. Bob Hall in Milwaukee, Wisconsin, was running the unit, and I had the privilege of choosing what unit I wanted to work on. Bob said to me, "You really need to know about alcoholism. What have you learned about it?" And I said, "Nothing." And he said, "Well, this is the second most common diagnosis any clinician is going to see in their practice, and a psychologist can make a life-or-death difference in this; it's important, so come on in and learn about it." So, I took his advice and did.

One thing that was breaking that summer was the work of the Sobells [Editor's note: for more on this controversy and the work of the Sobells, see Stanton Peele's informational article at www.peele.net/lib/glass]. Bob didn't know too much about it, but he handed me this document from Patton State Hospital and said, "Read this and see if there's anything you think we should be doing." I studied the document, and we discovered that we had actually tried out a little bit of that - controlled drinking - on the unit during that summer (1973). By the end of the summer, I believe we had concluded that this was not going to be a particularly promising approach with the folks who were in this unit; the severity level was such that this probably wasn't the way to go. But it got me thinking.

I went back to Oregon thinking I'd like to catch people further upstream, before they've gone over the waterfall - which is just what I had seen on the unit in Wisconsin. I wanted to go upstream a ways and try to help people *manage* their drinking before it got so out of control and has such a devastating effect on their lives. I really thought this idea was more indicative of prevention or secondary prevention and so put together a program aimed at helping people to moderate their drinking, which in those days had the term "controlled drinking" that has lots of over-meanings that are problematic. But, essentially, the goal of this program was to find people who were drinking too much, who were willing to make a change in it and help them get it down to a level that wasn't medically or psychologically harmful to them or to the people around them. And that's what I designed my dissertation around. I tested out three different ways of helping people moderate their drinking based on the literature that was available at the time.

One of those methods was essentially behavioral counseling, teaching people how to regulate their own behavior by giving them some practical tips with tools like self-monitoring, identifying triggers, changing their topography of drinking so they're not drinking so quickly, choosing less-preferred beverages – ideas right out of Weight Watcher's basically. The second one was aversion therapy. At the time, electrical aversion therapy looked promising in the literature and, indeed, I think it does help people reduce their drinking. However, it's doggoned unpleasant, so it's not a therapy that's ever going to grow in popularity much, but we tried it. And the third one was really modeled on the work of Lovibond [Editor's note: See "Reduced-risk drinking as a treatment goal: what clinicians need to know", *Journal of Substance Abuse Treatment*, Volume 22, Issue 1, pages 45-53] and the Sobells and was a much more extensive training. We actually built a bar and had people come in and practice moderate drinking. We included the aversive counter-conditioning component that was in the Lovibond work and gave people blood and breath alcohol feedback: the whole nine yards. We then compared these three in randomized trials. What we found, essentially, was that the outcomes were very similar in all three: somewhat less good outcomes for the electrical aversion therapy; but basically sitting in a room without a bar, without electrodes, without drinks or anything and talking to people about ways to regulate their behavior was working as well as the most extensive thing that we could do. The surprise that came out of all this was that people also seemed to benefit from the self-help materials that we put together.

In essence, I had been feeling guilty about just focusing so much on drinking and not on the other parts of people's lives - my training had been more broad-spectrum – and so with a colleague Ricardo Munoz (co-author of *Controlling Your Drinking*[49] with Bill Miller and a leading expert on depression) wrote a little handbook that both had the tips that we were telling people for managing their drinking but also some little tips about managing depression or mood and anxiety, sleep problems, and other things that go along with it, thinking that at least we'd given them something helpful. Then my dissertation advisor, Ed Liechtenstein, said, "Well, you'd better be careful that you're not messing up your outcomes by giving this booklet to people." So we decided to randomly assign people at the end of treatment to get or not get this little self-help book. Then we followed these folks for three more months to make sure it didn't have an effect on outcome and found - it did! Indeed, people who got the self-help book continued to decrease their drinking over time, and those who didn't get the self-help book were flat: that is, they stayed where they were at the end of treatment; they didn't go back to pre-treatment levels, but they also didn't get any better. "Well," I thought, "that's interesting!" So, we designed another study.

In this study, people were randomized to come in to see a therapist for ten weeks and get this behavioral counseling that was working well in the first study, or they were just given this self-help material and told to go home and try it and we'd see them again in ten weeks to see how they were doing. To my surprise and horror, the two groups did equally well! As a matter of fact, the group working on their own seemed to have a steeper decline in their drinking! This was the beginning of all the brief intervention materials, and eventually Motivational Interviewing, that emerged over time by following the data. But those were the first two studies that I did. And we got good results. People substantially reduced their drinking from what were risky levels, levels that pretty clearly were going to get them in trouble if they hadn't already. They got their drinking down to levels that were, if not what we would even call moderate drinking these days, pretty close to it: a reduction in drinking of more than 50%. So, from that I came away with a sense that here was something that we can do that is really a treatment for a population that had no previous treatment available – that is, people who are problem drinkers or less severe folks, but people who wouldn't go near a treatment center and don't find themselves at home in Alcoholics Anonymous but, nonetheless, are drinking in a way that's going to get them in trouble if it isn't already. So I followed that thread for some 10-15 years trying to refine the treatment methods and verify that the self-help approach was indeed working: we did that in five studies and, in all five studies, people working on their own did just as well as those seeing a therapist.

Then we began looking at the therapists. We began to see that some therapists were doing much better than the self-help book - though some were doing much worse and some just the same. When we averaged all the therapists together, we got the same outcome. But, in fact, *individual therapists* differed significantly from the outcome of the self-help book group such that some of these therapists were consistently getting more improvement in patients than when patients worked on their own. Yet, in other cases, the patient would have been better off going home with a good book! We discovered that it was the averaging across therapists that created the mistaken idea that therapists aren't different from self-help books, whereas they are - sometimes in a good direction and sometimes in a less good direction. The thing that differentiated the better therapists from the less good therapists was *empathy*. The Truax/Carkhuff scale [Editor's note: *www.sageofasheville.com/pub_downloads/EMPATHIC_UNDERSTANDING.pdf*, p4, for more information on Carkhuff's revision of Truax's scale] was just a dandy predictor of which therapists were going to have a high success rate doing behavior therapy. This was the seed that sent me off on sabbatical in 1982, which kind of gave birth to Motivational Interviewing. So that was my early history with harm reduction - or moderation, or controlled drinking or whatever you want to call it.

We did have other interesting findings from some long-term follow-ups I did also. There was a psychiatrist here in town [Editor's note: Albuquerque, NM], a smart guy who was giving talks and being fairly critical of the work we were doing, essentially saying "it can't work." So we invited him to come and collaborate in an outcome study in which both he and I would, independently, interview all the patients we had seen in four different studies and come to a conclusion about what the outcome was; put our heads together and see if we could agree about it, and we did agree on what the outcomes were that we were seeing. I think we were both surprised by the outcomes: he was surprised to see that yes, indeed, there are people here with moderate problem-free drinking conditions that they are maintaining well over time, and I was surprised that there were fewer of them than we thought and that many more people had actually decided – on their own - to quit drinking.

These were folks who said that the controlled drinking program had helped them to decide to quit drinking. They had tried the controlled drinking in our study and indeed, from our criteria, they had been successful at doing it: they had gotten their drinking down. What they said was that it was just too hard; it was like 'white-knuckle' moderation! They said they felt like they were hanging on for dear life and they could fall off at any time. It was simply too much work to moderate and just easier to abstain plus, as they said, "When I was drinking moderately, it was like what's the point? I drink to get high!" For them, the value of drinking moderately was very low, and the struggle to maintain it was very high. As a result, quite a few people quit drinking and, again, often they attributed their decision to do so to having tried this moderation approach and finding it too hard. These were some of the surprises that came out of the follow-up studies.

You know, we really just wanted to see what would happen if people were invited to empirically look at their drinking – without feeling like they were in prison and *couldn't* drink – to look at their goals around drinking, to see what happened when they tried to obtain those drinking goals. We thought, at worst, they would figure out that this moderation isn't something that works for them and they would then have this information. We asked people in the beginning of the program what their goal was, and the goal of some of the people – right from the beginning - was to abstain, to our surprise. Many endorsed the second goal we had which was:

"I'd like to moderate my drinking but if I found that I couldn't, then I'd like to abstain." And almost all of those folks abstained, interestingly. The third goal was: "I want to moderate my drinking; I don't want to abstain." Many of those folks wound up moderating, too. So even from an initial question regarding people's goals, we could sort out where people were likely going to wind up.

Another interesting finding from our long-term follow up is this: the abstainers - the people who were non-drinkers - many of them did drink somewhere along the line, but almost invariably they would have a drink or two and maybe the next day have a drink or two, and then they would say, "This is stupid; why am I doing this?" and go back to abstaining. We suddenly realized that we weren't seeing the huge relapses that were so characterized in the literature. Choosing their own goal was almost an inoculation or something because they knew moderation was there - and they tried it and didn't blow the top off their drinking, but there just wasn't any joy in it; you know, sort of a "why do this?" attitude. But they would have these little tiny slips, you might say, and then go back to abstinence for years after that. In a way, this individual goal-setting put a cap on the severity of the relapse, or so it appeared. Again, very different from what we expected.

So I think of harm reduction as simply a goal. In that sense, it's one that's pretty hard not to sign onto as a clinician because I certainly hope that the work that I do involves reducing the amount of harm that comes to the people that I work with and those around them. However you think about treatment, most likely what you're hoping to do is at least to reduce the harm that happens and, perhaps, to promote well-being and happiness and things way beyond that. But that's a general goal of clinical work, too, so to me that's non-controversial. What has gotten controversial about the words "harm reduction" in the United States is particular practices or methods - that's where folks begin to disagree. But I hope we have a common meeting ground around the idea that what we're trying to do is to prevent or reduce the amount of harm that happens to people we serve and those around them. Often, these disagreements are in gradual versus binary approaches. The most obvious of those is "abstinence now" versus "'no change" as a binary approach or "steps in the right direction," which is more often associated with the term "harm reduction."

It has always seemed sensible to me that "steps in the right direction" is what one would want to do because human beings aren't perfect and, if an individual is able to make a turnabout, "our hats are off to them" as is said in AA, but most people most of the time don't make changes in an absolute kind of way. We're not all quantum changers; most of us most of the time change a little bit at a time. Indeed, big commitments tend to happen small steps at a time. So helping people take what steps they are able and willing to take at a particular time has *always* made sense to me. From the very beginning of my work in the 1970s with alcohol problems, that's just what seemed to me a no-brainer, so that wasn't a conversion for me. It wasn't that I did something different previously and saw the error of my ways and began to do this. For me, my training as a behavioral psychologist, where you have people who make successful approximations to goals – that's a normal thing you do – it just seemed the natural thing you would do with alcohol problems.

Today, I just keep following my data, which continue to show me that treating people with respect and listening to their goals – this Rogerian way of being with people – is what really works in helping people make changes in their lives. And Motivational Interviewing is the vehicle, it seems, to guide people in deciding to make these changes that they desire and in ways that work for them. What's great about Motivational Interviewing is that it can be used within any theoretical framework: harm reduction, 12-Step, or something else. It's not in a camp. Just as I wouldn't label MI as a strictly harm reduction-friendly style, I continue to resist being labeled as only a harm reductionist; again, that's a little confining thimble that is a very small piece of what I do. I just don't like labels – period!

William (Bill) R. Miller is Emeritus Distinguished Professor of Psychology and Psychiatry at the University of New Mexico, Albuquerque, NM. Although retired from academia, Dr. Miller continues his work on Motivational Interviewing through research, lecture, workshops, and writing. He can be reached at <u>wrmiller@unm.edu</u>.

LISA MOORE

HARM REDUCTION OLDTIMER

When I look back on some of my beginnings in harm reduction, I remember some of the wonderful craziness and not-so wonderful nastiness in some work groups I was attending around harm reduction issues. But you know, those early beginnings remind *me* not to be utterly dogmatic about things either because there is a definite muddiness between being highly committed and being over-the-top. I know I've slipped into over-the-top on occasion - hopefully less often rather than more - but I think we all have the tendency to do it when we are really involved in something we believe in.

Also, I think we flip out depending on how fragile we are individually. I have a couple of dear friends who are still very old school AA. I always said to them - while trying to not be disrespectful - that part of this is defensiveness, that they apparently feel their sobriety is fragile. Now, I also really don't want to mess with that sobriety, so if it *is* fragile, by all means do what you need to do to handle it! There just seems to be a feeling of fragility of minds regardless of which side of the fence people are on: abstinence or harm reduction. Sometimes it almost feels like it's all gonna crack if you were to let in anything else. I think this is what people on both sides of this issue are most afraid of: the cracking of their beliefs and perhaps, therefore, of themselves somehow.

People feel that they can control things if the lines are clearly delineated – like abstinence: you either are or you aren't abstinent. Yet there really is no way to control something even if the lines are delineated, but apparently nobody has told them that yet! Again, if this is how you need to think about things to turn your life around, then that's OK, but at some point - because the world isn't black and white – that thinking has to shift, and you have to find a way to make the shift to figure out on what terms you're going to live your life, right?

What's interesting to me about AA is that - and it's probably true sometimes and other times not – it hasn't built-in a way for a member to *leave* the program, including a building-up of social support that may be sober or simply supportive even if it isn't AA support, like treatment would (think "continuing care"). This seems to be part of how AA gets dichotomized: either you're hanging out with people who are "clean and sober" or you're hanging out with a bunch of people at a bar: no middle ground. It's not like, "here are your tools because what you need to do is set up a life where you can be sober no matter where you are or who you're with, which naturally includes people who will support you when you're sober." To me, this shift from a past kind of life to a different, hopefully healthier one, needs to be a constant transition that people must make. And those supportive people may or may not be in AA, but they'd probably need to be other people making healthier changes in their lives. Because you are not going to maintain sobriety if everybody you're hanging out with is strung out, I don't care who you are! If you work in a bakery with all sugar-heads and you don't want to eat sugar, well, it's the same thing: it's going to be pretty tough to stay away from sugar! It's important to have people - coworkers, community, whomever - support you whenever you make changes in your life.

In this conversation about harm reduction and AA, it also seems important to look at the language we use. This whole idea of "clean" and "dirty" really bothers me. I mean, what does that mean anyway? Most forms of internalized oppression operate the same way, with this kind of covert language attached to things. When I was a kid, black people in my grandmother's generation talked about whether you had "good hair" or "bad hair" (bad hair being more African). Of course, those of us with so-called "good hair" were thought to be prettier than those with "bad hair." Likewise is this idea that a person who uses drugs is "dirty:" dirt is bad and drugs are bad, so drug *users* are bad, right? At least real dirt you can see but this is a kind of insidious, invisible dirt – it's like an infection, isn't it? Like something just under the skin, below the surface that can wreak havoc. It's just horrible the way we talk about, and therefore think about, drug users. To me, it's very similar to making racial undertones based on superficial skin color. And it's really about the fact that you're different somehow underneath - that you don't have the same heart or soul or importance. Your intrinsic value therefore is less.

This is a problem in public health in general. I remember when I was in graduate school, a woman named Caroline Wang wrote this paper talking about how there were materials being produced by people who wanted to get folks to comply with helmet laws. To do so, they were using images of brain-injured people: "Don't use a helmet and this can happen to you!" Ms. Wang pointed out that in order to encourage people to use helmets the producers were accidentally encouraging the stigmatization of brain-injured people, right? They were basically saying, "look at what a horrible mess *this* person is. You don't wanna be like them, right?" They weren't being that vulgar about it, but that's basically what they're saying. We do that all the time in public health: "You don't wanna be like that person because they're sickly - they're this, they're that; they're less than you so you're gonna do what we tell you to do. Basically, if you don't wanna be scum *like them*, you follow Public Health mandates." We are so unconscious about how we stigmatize. I think that AA and drug use treatment and policies are some of the more egregious ways we stigmatize because, in this case, we decide to put this whole criminal justice apparatus with it and conflate it with all this race and class crap. It's totally egregious, but I don't think it's out of the ordinary; it's just to what degree? And that's been one of my obsessions about what's screwed up about public health in general - either you're healthy or you're scum.

Just how do we achieve *recovery* when the way that we define it is to "'not be scum?" That's pretty insidious to me. We absolutely need to redefine recovery. To me, recovery is not engaging in hateful behavior towards oneself and others. Not at all from a Judeo-Christian stance, just a kind of "are you doing right by yourself and other people?" and most of us aren't. I don't do it to the degree I'd like to. And yet, how hard do we need to try to "do right?" How hard does life have to get before we can be gentler to ourselves and others? How hard is "hard enough," who deserves such treatment and who gets to decide? For some of us, I don't think we *ever* feel like our lives are hard enough to warrant thinking we should be generous to ourselves; there's always somebody who is worse off than us!

As to defining harm reduction, or the difference between harm reduction and abstinence, I do think that abstinence is arguably healthier for most people. And so is exercising seven days a week and not being stressed and all those other things that we are never going to achieve perfectly in this society in my lifetime! So, why is harm reduction policy a problem? Isn't it better to accept that eating one salad a week is better than never eating any greens at all? I guess to me this is the basis of my idea of harm reduction, which doesn't come out of any kind of drug thing because I never was professionally in the drug world, but my *profession* was in the drug world. It's funny because I think that's part of why I never got really into the drug world much; I got into harm reduction through HIV. But no matter the route, I do want people – *all* people - to be healthier and happier on some level. Besides, if I were truly able to be hedonistic in the proper way - truly enjoying what I was doing instead of having all this other guilt associated with it - then I don't think I would be engaging in dysfunctional drug use; I'd be more mindful.

That being said, it's always been my experience and belief that we all have so much baggage that one doesn't always have a lot of control over one's ability to be mindful. I mean, we'd like to be more mindful than we are, but sometimes things come up that we don't expect, and we become rather mindless about all kinds of things in our lives, let alone alcohol and other drug use. To me, in the best of all possible worlds, the kind of drug use that would be happening would be *mindful drug use*. I remember reading years and years ago about ritual and anthropology, and one of the things that interested me was the idea of how various cultures (including Americans to some degree in the mid-1850s to 1900s) have used substances ritualistically and not addictively [Editor's note: see *From Morphine to Chocolate, Revised Edition (2004)* by Andrew Weil, MD, & Winifred Rosen (Houghton Mifflin Co) for an engaging discussion of this phenomenon]. And of course, drug use today in the US is especially different from what we see in other cultures.

Today in the US, I see drinking as the best example of the use of a drug that is markedly different here than in other cultures. When you go to different countries and see how people drink there, it's vastly different than here; and that's when the light bulb went off for me. I remember going to France when I was about 19 and, yeah, they have liver problems, but they also have a different concept of drinking, and that was remarkable to me. Generally, Europeans drink at a younger age (diluted and ritualized with meals, etc.), but they drink more responsibly as well. That's certainly much different than what we see here in the States.

Coming to Harm Reduction Kicking & Screaming

We also need to remember the biases we have in our studies in the States. Like in epidemiology where we have a *hospital bias*. It's one of the things they teach you when you're taking those courses. The upshot of it is researchers were doing all these studies in *hospitals* and, all of a sudden, some genius realized that they were being a bunch of nimrods because the people were *in* hospitals because they were sick – therefore not well - so that's the bias – you're only looking at people who are already sick if you look at only people in hospitals! So, if we are going to sample people from hospitals, mental institutions, jails, wherever, people are going to be experiencing "issues" likely different from your standard population, right? I think this bias has led us to some of the greatest policy errors that we have completely overlooked with drug users: most drug users end up in *jail*, not in hospitals, and they also don't end up in treatment settings. In other words, we're basing our policies - and even treatment decisions - on studies that look at people who wind up in *jail* not in *treatment*, which is the wrong population group!

In this really old book about treatment, *Pathways From Heroin Addiction*[50] by Pat Biernacki, one of the things the author discussed was that he interviewed a bunch of people who stopped using drugs - or at least stopped using them in destructive or dysfunctional ways – and that these were folks who had never gone through formal drug treatment. He looked at whether they had social support that was organized through non drug-taking behaviors and whether this social support would produce a positive outcome regarding their drug use: in other words, could these folks stop on their own as long as they had social support? In people who lost their jobs, lost their families and their communities and for whom the only support they had was their other friends who were users, the outcome was dismal. But the folks who could go back to their families or go back to their jobs, they did well. That made a lot of sense to me - and surprised me as well.

At one point, when I was in grad school, my life had gotten really out of control, and I experienced what I think of as the ultimate bourgeois drug treatment. I was working for Urban Health Studies doing interviews, and people would ask me, "Have you ever had any problems with drugs?" and I'd say, "Yeah" and they'd ask, "Did you ever shoot drugs?" and I'd say, "Yeah" and they'd say, "Really, what'd you do to stop?" And I'd say, "I just stopped because I went to graduate school and got away from who I was." Everybody would kind of look at me strangely, but for me, "treatment" was just that I found a way to have a clean break with what I'd been doing before – that's one of the ultimate privileges, being able to go to grad school. It was grad school that gave me a chance to meet a group of people that didn't know me in my "party central" mode. I got a chance to rethink how I was going to be in the world, and I think that was what was so cool about harm reduction: I took this break from drug use and went to grad school and hung out with all these nerds and then eventually kinda came out to them and to myself about how I'm a nerd, and I'm also all this other stuff. Then when harm reduction came around (I started grad school in 1986) and I began working in it (in 1988), my work became one of the healthiest things that could've happened to me. Instead of having to divorce myself from what I'd been up to all those years and pretend that the drug user part of me didn't exist, I could say, "No, that's me, too. And I can hang out in the streets and talk to folks because I've been on the streets, too; I can talk to people who some of y'all couldn't talk to if you wanted to because drug users just won't trust you like they will me!" Plus I think I'm good at studying the street user partly because I am a nerd, but mostly because I am a drug-using nerd. Put that in your pipe and smoke it! I was forced to make this separation of my selves, and then I got to integrate them again! I also got a chance to not be ashamed of it because I had been ashamed of my two selves. Now I realize that I don't have to be ashamed of who I really am because, by being a drug user at some point in my life, I've learned things about being in the world that other people don't know, things that you can't read in a book. I wish everybody had those opportunities to combine street knowledge and book knowledge. I guess that would be part of my idea of recovery: that you can stop being ashamed of who you are or were, realize the value in your knowledge and self, and turn it all into something positive for yourself and the world. Now, that's true harm reduction!

Lisa Moore is Associate Professor at San Francisco State University, Department of Health Education. She can be reached through her website there at http://userwww.sfsu.edu/~lisadee/

STANTON PEELE

ORIGINAL HARM REDUCTION OLDTIMER

I have to say I didn't discover harm reduction; harm reduction discovered me. I believe that while I am a pioneer in harm reduction, I don't think of myself as *working* in harm reduction. My work in addiction and harm reduction is just a natural consequence to understanding what addiction is. If addiction is a particular problem people have in the way they live, the problem being that they've become completely enmeshed in one experience, then the answer to that is to change your relationship to life. That statement - "changing your relationship to life" - indicates that change is an incremental process. You don't one day wake up and suddenly you're not addicted; you make changes in your life, you evolve, you mature, you think different things, your life becomes more fulfilling. Another of my recent books, called *7 Tools to Beat Addiction* (Three Rivers Press, 2004), is about the ordinary things in life that you have at your disposal that enable you to get out of an addiction, to improve your life and with it reduce your addictiveness. So, just the very way I've approached addiction, beginning in 1975 with my book called *Love & Addiction* (with Archie Brodsky; Signet, 1976), implies and is based on a kind of harm reduction model. My 1991 book, *The Truth About Addiction and Recovery* (Fireside, 1992), is the first clinical harm reduction handbook, which other harm reductionists like Patt Denning and Edith Springer later picked up on.

I wrote *Diseasing of America* in 1989 (Jossey-Bass, 1999), which is probably when I became known as Mr. Anti-12-Step. In 1975 when I wrote *Love & Addiction,* the real myth that I was combating was the myth of heroin addiction, which is still around. The myth is when you take heroin you become addicted instantly. This suggests that this has nothing to do with you: it's the drug that is addictive itself. In *Love & Addiction,* I announce there are a few things wrong with this thinking; in fact, *everything* about it is wrong. For example, a lot of people take narcotics without getting addicted. Think of all those hospital patients for instance. At the time I wrote *Love & Addiction*, people didn't think that cigarettes were addictive. We just didn't think that way, which goes to show how so much of what we think about addiction is culturally and historically determined. An idea gets out there, and then people have this idea. So, the idea I was combating when I wrote *Love & Addiction* was this platonic ideal of addiction: heroin equaled addiction. I knew in my gut that this ideal was wrong. I had a PhD in social psychology, and felt I had an understanding of how people work and what influences them: for example, people are influenced by the people around them. And some social psychologists had looked at this influence while doing research on drugs and found that people tended to take drugs the way that people they knew take drugs; they drank the way they knew people around them drank.

From the start I was a contrarian, somebody who didn't go along with the accepted concepts of addiction, although at the time I wasn't fighting AA and the 12-Steps so much as I was fighting this platonic ideal of addiction as this perfect codifiable trait that rose from one drug really: heroin. You can't reduce addiction down to this one thing, this *reductionist* way of thinking: heroin causes addiction. It just doesn't make sense.

There's a feeling afoot that there's been a revolution in addictive thinking, put forth by Nora Volkow who's the current director of NIDA [Editor's note: National Institute of Drug Abuse; see www.nida.nih.org] and a very talented person. Now, she's constantly beating the drum that we're on the verge of curing addiction. We're looking at the brain in terms of MRIs and people are thinking, "now we've really got the cure for addiction in hand!" They're wrong. To highlight this, one thing I like to do - even when I talk to addiction researchers - is ask a group to whom I'm speaking, "Do you think there is going to be the same amount of addiction in 20 years, less addiction or more addiction?" Virtually everyone thinks there's going to be more addiction, even some of the same researchers who are looking for the cure. Why? Because deep down everybody knows that Nora Volkow is wrong; everybody knows that addiction is something much more complex than some individual brain reaction you can nip in the bud if you can only locate it in the brain. How is this happening? Because the label "'science" has been applied to medical technology, people think this is the science of addiction - looking in the place that neurotransmitters and parts of the brain are firing when a drug is used - and that will be the cure for addiction! It just seems so much more old-fashioned and not really scientific to say, "well, that's not how people become addicted; that's not how people overcome addiction." These discoveries, while interesting, really have nothing to do with the prevalence of or cure for addiction. If you take an MRI of any person who uses cocaine, you see their pleasure center light up. But only *some* of those people become addicted to using cocaine. Some people get exactly the same amount of pleasure as an addict - maybe their brain lights up even more - and yet they get up in the morning and say, "well, you know, I have to go to work; I've got these three children. I don't want to be a cocaine addict. Last night was last night and that's it." People make choices like that constantly. I'm not going to debate free will. However, you can say something about people who are less likely to become addicted by looking at the life they're imbedded in: they often have a job and a family, which are anti-addictive mechanisms. They're not perfect anti-addictive mechanisms, but they're better anti-addictive elements than any drug anyone will ever invent. Having a full life fights addiction!

On this same topic, I have a new book called *Addiction-Proof Your Child* (Three Rivers Press, 2007), and I say that parents are the most critical element to whether someone becomes addicted. And I think that everyone knows this. Oh, someone will say, "You're either born to be an addict or not," and yet everybody knows the meaning and the significance of the term "high-risk kid." Before they ever heard Nora Volkow lecture, they knew the truth: people know that if you're in a bad place, if there's abuse in your house, if you get off on the wrong foot, if you don't deal with school, well, this fertilizes the crop from which most substance abusers come. And almost everybody knows that the single best thing that you can do to help adolescents predisposed to addiction not become addicted is to get them engaged in a mainstream (for want of a better word) life. Get them interested in some kind of work to develop normal relationships, to see themselves as able to be satisfied and to cope with the world.   Now, I'm not saying that something can't happen to this child to get them off track, which leads to their becoming dependent. But it is a cumulative effect of a lot of little things. And it started somewhere in the home virtually always.

Let's look at how the DSM[51] looks at addiction. The DSM calls addiction "drug or alcohol *dependence."* But if you ask people this question, "Are children today more or less dependent than your generation were?" everybody says, "More." That's because it's considered normal upbringing for a child today to be protected into dependence well into their 20s. Things that ordinary, regular middle-class people used to do, you'd sort of get arrested for today. Like saying to a ten-year-old, "Why don't you take the bus to the swimming pool in town?" That would be considered potential child abuse now, i.e. putting them at risk. Yet, as much as we watch on Fox News that kids are being molested, it still doesn't happen that much. Really, your child is much more likely to harm themselves through things they become involved in on their own or in their own home. Beyond this, if you were to ask what is the single-most important thing a human being can do so they won't wind up addicted or *dependent*, it's the ability to be *independent*. That's not that complicated; you don't have to go to school to see that. What the opposite of dependence – this *independence* - involves is facing life on your own, in graduated steps: dealing with challenges. And you're going to both succeed and fail. You might scrape your knees, but you'll learn from that and scrape your knees less. You'll develop skills that will lead to the most important thing that you'll develop: a feeling of self-efficacy, of being able to say to yourself: "You know, something's going to come up here that's going to be tough to handle, but I *can* handle it." Addiction, on the other hand, is most often prompted when people face something stressful and say to themselves, "Oh God, what am I going to do? I can't handle this. I can't deal with whatever is being thrown at me." That's a bad feeling, and it's hard to "cure" when you're in your 20s, 30s, 40s, etc. But in a normal development, children learn, quite early on, that feeling of self-efficacy, which is protective against their likelihood of developing a drug dependence.

One thing that helps people set limits to their use of substances is when they are doing something for a specific purpose. In other words, what's the difference between a heroin addict and the person who goes to the hospital and gets painkillers? Well, the hospital patient is getting the painkillers for *pain*: they know specifically why they're taking it. For a long time, hospitals were worried about patients becoming addicted while hospitalized, and so it took a long time to develop the policy of allowing patients to self-medicate with narcotics [Editor's note: this is accomplished through the use of a PCA - Patient Controlled Analgesia - a mechanized self-regulating, and self-administered, pump used in most hospitals today typically to dispense morphine to patients]. Surprisingly, they found that people use less of a narcotic when they self-medicate than when they were given narcotics by medical personnel! This is because, given the right opportunity, people tend to use things for specific reasons and, when the reasons change, they don't use it anymore. We're really looking here at how a human being relates to the *experience* of taking a drug rather than just the drug itself [Editor's note: for more on this concept, see *Drug, Set, Setting: The Basis for Controlled Intoxicant Use,* Norman Zinberg, MD, Yale University Press, 1986]. And so we're also really talking about harm reduction because we're talking about the unique and important parts of one's experience with a drug: that a drug does X when you're at one place in life and does Y when you're in yet another.

For me, harm reduction is non-abstinent improvement in the lives of addicted people. This can lead to abstinence or, at least, abstinence from one drug. I do not think that harm reduction includes abstinence, only because it doesn't need to: people already know about abstinence. In fact, abstinence has been so oversold as the "answer" to addiction that the notion of abstinence as the only resolution to addiction is dangerous. It so rarely occurs, yet it crowds out everything else that human beings can do to improve their lives, like needle exchange, or using narcotics in safer forms, or cutting back, even if your use is still harmful. Drinking less often or only at home can eliminate dangerous criminal and sexual activity. You may still be "addicted," but there's no question you've improved your life and the lives of those around you. And that is good; and that is harm reduction.

Stanton Peele is the author of numerous books on addiction, treatment, society, and more. His latest is *"7 Tools to Beat Addiction"* (Three Rivers Press, 2004). He can be reached through his website at www.peele.net.

FRED ROTGERS

HARM REDUCTION OLDTIMER

Early on, when I first started working with people with alcohol and drug problems, I was working in a prison and I ran a therapeutic community inside the walls of the local State Prison. This was one of the first efforts to actually do a therapeutic community (TC) inside a correctional setting. Now, of course, that's virtually all the addiction treatment offenders get, if they get any treatment at all while in prison. As I had received very little training in addictions during my training as a psychologist, this "treatment-in-prison" wound up being my indoctrination to addiction treatment. This meant that I was pretty much in an abstinence-only mode although I was never completely rigid about that. Still, my thinking didn't fully change to harm reduction until some years later.

    I don't remember exactly when it was, but my initial turning point (there were a few) toward full harm reduction was when I went to a conference in New York where one of the speakers was this young, up-and-coming psychologist named Alan Marlatt, and he was talking about relapse prevention. One of the things he talked about was this concept he called "programmed relapses." What he meant by this was the idea that once someone had achieved abstinence, they might begin to test their newfound sobriety skills and intentionally use their substance of choice in a safe context by using all the skills they learned in treatment, a model he called "Cognitive Behavioral Relapse Prevention." I'll never forget watching as a number of people stood up in the audience accusing him of killing people as he spoke more about this model. They were actually yelling at him, saying the only way to get better was with AA and abstaining completely from all mind-altering substances - the whole radical conservative abstinence-only stance, what I call "the Smithers-NCADD position" [Editor's note: In 1952, R. Brinkley Smithers founded the Christopher D. Smithers Foundation "to educate the American public on the respectable and treatable disease of alcoholism." For more information, see www.smithersfoundation.org; NCADD is the National Council on Alcoholism and Drug Dependence. See www.ncadd.org for more]. It was unbelievable! I remember knowing at that point my abstinence-only thinking was gone forever - period, full stop. A number of years later, Alan was the president of what was then the AABT (the Association for the Advancement of Behavior Therapy, now the Association for Behavioral and Cognitive Therapy) and, in his presidential address at the end of his term, he spoke about harm reduction for the first time. That was also the first time I heard the term "harm reduction" mentioned publicly. So first Alan had discussed this controversial concept of "programmed relapses" and now it was harm reduction; my mind was blown by these concepts! I was definitely on my way to being a fully-fledged harm reductionist.

Around this time, I became the Director of the Training Clinic at the Center of Alcohol Studies (CAS) at Rutgers University and was familiarizing myself with the moderate drinking literature. I had heard of Bill Miller [Editor's note: co-author, *Motivational Interviewing*[52]; *Controlling Your Drinking*[53]], and was also familiar with Linda and Mark Sobell's landmark and controversial work[54] from my being a member of AABT (they were both past AABT presidents). Two other things happened, too: first, I met a woman named Diana McCague from New Brunswick, New Jersey who had started the first needle exchange in New Jersey (needle exchanges only became legal in New Jersey in 2007, becoming the last state in the Union where intravenous drug users can obtain sterile needles legally, for any purpose). Diana established the needle exchange by having numerous conversations with the New Brunswick police. She convinced the police chief that needle exchange made a difference to the health of their consumers. Diana was interested in getting training for her staff from our clinic on how to better talk to their consumers about possible treatment options if folks decided they wanted to change their drug use. Well, the needle exchange program ultimately was shut down, rather abruptly. The County Drug Task Force actually arrested Diana when the New Brunswick police chief was out on vacation. She, and the needle exchange, couldn't be protected without him. She wound up having a widely publicized trial at which Ernie Drucker [Editor's note: founded the International Harm Reduction Association in 1995; see www.ihra.net], Don DesJarlais [Editor's note: current Director of Research at the Baron Edmond de Rothschild Chemical Dependency Institute at Beth Israel Medical Center, in New York City, and more. See www.opiateaddictionrx.info/about/desjarlais.html for more on Dr. DesJarlais] and I testified since we were all people involved with harm reduction and needle exchange. Interestingly enough, at the end of Diana's trial, the judge said to her, "If I had a daughter I'd want her to be like you." But laws are strange. She managed to stay out of jail but lost her driver's license - one of the odd consequences of New Jersey's drug laws – and the needle exchange was closed.

The second thing that happened right around this same time was that Jon Morgenstern [Editor's note: Dr. Morgenstern is currently the Director of Treatment Research at the Center on Addictions and Substance Abuse at Columbia University and Associate Professor of Psychiatry at Mt. Sinai School of Medicine in New York] and I began to look through the research literature to see if there was a group of problem drinkers who were essentially not receiving services for their problematic, not *alcoholic*, drinking patterns. We focused our search on research on folks who were simply problem drinkers (non-dependent) to see what research said was the best treatment option(s) for them. And what did it say? *Moderate drinking*. There was a surprisingly large amount of research on moderate drinking. So much so that in 2000, in an article in the *Journal for Studies on Alcohol*, Nick Heather made the statement that Behavioral Self-Control Training (Bill Miller's Moderation Program) was the single most studied intervention for alcohol problems and the one with the most evidence for its effectiveness. That was in 2000, mind you; we knew that moderation worked with simple problem drinkers. So why isn't this program being used?

Well, I believe that one of the major reasons is because addiction counselors often don't receive this research information: they don't know it exists nor that it works. When I tell people about this kind of moderation research, they can't believe it. At a training of mine recently, a participant who is a former nurse now taking addictions courses for certification said, "I've heard of Motivational Interviewing (MI), but I was wondering, is this something new?" I couldn't believe it. I informed her that not only is it not new, but that the first article about MI was published in 1983, though the very fact that she can ask "is this new?" indicates how poorly researchers have done at disseminating the fruits of all the research that the Federal Government has funded, let alone moderation research. In part, this is due to politics leading to the Federal Government's unwillingness to talk about things like "moderation training." They even refuse to fund research that has the words "harm reduction" explicitly stated in the project name, and yet they fund MI, which has harm reduction roots. It's all politics. Anyway, back to our search for research on this dramatically underserved population of people with drinking problems.

We also found epidemiological data that showed that, by some estimates, 20-25% of all drinkers in the US fell into this group: problem but not alcoholic drinkers. 20-25%! We're talking a big percentage here. And these were the sort of people for whom drinking definitely causes problems, like DUI's or family problems related to drinking too much. But they're not meeting the DSM (Editor's note: *Diagnostic and Statistical Manual*, now in its fourth edition; used in the health fields to diagnose mental health conditions including substance abuse and dependence) criteria for dependence, and they certainly would never go to a traditional treatment program where lifelong abstinence is the only goal because they correctly don't see their drinking problem as *alcoholic*. So what could we do for these underserved yet needy folks to give them some type of treatment without its being abstinence-based, which they would summarily reject? The faculty at CAS decided we would start a new type of treatment program for this problem-drinking population based around Bill Miller's *Drinker's Check Up* [Editor's note: The Drinker's Check Up was developed by Reid Hester and Bill Miller at the University of New Mexico, Albuquerque, and can be found at www.drinkerscheckup.com]. And so we did. Then the trouble really started.

The University was excited about this idea at this point and sent out press releases to all the local newspapers, including the New York papers, and in early 1995 a reporter from the New York Times contacted me. She was doing an article about this new support movement called Moderation Management, and she had just interviewed the founder Audrey Kishline to discuss her book,

Moderate Drinking: The Moderation Management (MM) Guide for People Who Want to Reduce Their Drinking (Three Rivers Press, 1995). Apparently our press release had landed on her desk, and she wanted to interview me for the article to get a professional opinion on moderation. Now, Audrey's Moderation Management (MM) program really took harm reduction into a new direction. It was quite popular back then, but mostly vilified by treatment professionals and by many 12-Steppers due to the inaccurate information that was often given about MM, especially in the media. Even though the evidence for moderation was there, politics was keeping it from getting out accurately into the mainstream.

This is also when I really began to see how these politics were beginning to creep into my own work at CAS more and more. For example, we have a building named Brinkley and Adele Smithers Hall at CAS. It is named for Adele and her husband Brinkley, who had been severely alcohol dependent and finally got sober through AA. When Brinkley died, Adele inherited both his fortune and the Smithers Foundation, which he had founded and which was a funding source for CAS. After she read the article in the New York Times about our new moderation program at CAS, she hit the roof and threatened to cut off our funding from The Smithers Foundation. Politics.

Another example of these politics led to the myth of how and why Audrey left Moderation Management. The myth was that she left after suffering an "inevitable" relapse on alcohol, leading to her arrest for driving under the influence of alcohol after having tragically killed two people with her car. The truth is that Audrey had left MM for AA several months before the accident, stating that she needed to find abstinence; she no longer felt moderate drinking was an option for her. But people started this rumor that "MM kills" due to this incident rather than accepting the truth that Audrey was actually in AA when the accident occurred. Eventually Audrey went to prison for her crime. [Editor's note: Audrey Kishline and Sheryl Maloy, the mother of one of her victims, have written a book about their joint healing titled, *Face to Face*]. Again, politics gets in the way of the facts. We live in the age of political spin, and this is a great, sad example of that.

It was around 1996 when I also met Andrew Tatarsky, Debbie Rothchild and Lisa Director, psychologists in New York, who had started the Mental Health Professionals in Harm Reduction group. I joined them and we sponsored the first major harm reduction conference in New York City. We expected to get perhaps 100 people; we got 300! We had people from the West Coast who were active in harm reduction and people who were doing harm reduction in New York. And it was here at this conference that I came full circle from my transformative beginnings with Alan's speeches to Diana's needle exchange work to looking at moderation research to CAS and our moderation program to Audrey and solidly into the next phase of harm reduction: clinical practice.

Gratefully, I have seen an increasing openness to harm reduction among treatment people even in the very conservative treatment world that's highbrow East Coast. People have started to look at the research and have come to the conclusion, as I did, that harm reduction is the only sensible approach to people's problem drug use. One of the reasons I think this is happening is that the level of education required of entry-level drug and alcohol counselors is now significantly higher. Because of this, they are getting exposed to ideas and concepts such as cognitive-behavioral approaches, Motivational Interviewing and more, and these evidence-based educated counselors are gradually getting treatment programs to adopt harm reduction principles. Treatment folks are seeing how these approaches help them to stop fighting with clients and that harm reduction makes their jobs easier. These new counselors are really changing things in traditional treatment. These new folks are often simply in this business because they want to help people, not just because they are in 12-Step recovery. They really want to find effective ways of helping people with problem behaviors solve their problems, and that's what I think we tap into when we rationally discuss harm reduction. Andrew Tatarsky has a nice little exercise that he does when he is talking to groups of counselors. He asks: "How many of you believe that in order to effectively engage someone in treatment and get them into recovery the person has to accept Step 1?" Of course all the hands go up. "So, if accepting Step 1 is critical, how many of you also believe that in order for your treatment to be effective people have to accept Step 1?" All the hands go up. "So, what treatment do you have for the people who don't accept Step 1?" The answer is "The door!" We know now that we have to do better than that for folks who want – and deserve - another way to change.

I really think things are changing, though gradually, through long talks with people to let them see that harm reduction truly reduces harm to people and that it includes abstinence when someone decides that's the best choice for their life. Let's be honest here - there are lots of ways that people get better: AA isn't the only one. Also, people rarely become abstinent in their first attempt, even in AA; it can take years - if it ever happens. We should practice true harm reduction in addiction treatment, meaning simply that we should be meeting people where they're at, helping them make healthier decisions about their lives in ways that make sense to them. Shouldn't we have *all* possible approaches available to them in order to best assure this? I certainly think so.

Fred Rotgers is currently Program Director for Clinical Psychology at Walden University. He can be reached at Frederick.Rotgers@email.waldenu.edu.

ANDREW TATARSKY
HARM REDUCTION OLDTIMER

I was trained in graduate school as a psychologist in a kind of integrative psychoanalytical perspective that honored the multiplicity of the different psychoanalytical perspectives as well as the value of cognitive-behavioral approaches. It was a way of thinking of human suffering and human problems in a very complex way that also showed the importance of individualizing any attempt to help people. I felt very lucky to be exposed to this kind of very interesting, diverse group of ideas. This was at the City College of New York Clinical Psychology program in the 1980s.

In the course of my training as a graduate student, I worked with some people who had problems with drugs and alcohol, but I never got any formal training in drug and alcohol counseling. Then, at an internship at King's County Hospital in Brooklyn, I saw some patients that had some problems with drugs and alcohol. Again, I never really got any formal training but, in trying to think of how to work with these folks from within the perspective that I had been trained in graduate school, there was some success but also a lot of bumbling.

Later, by what appeared at the time to be by accident (in retrospect I don't think it was completely by accident), I got my first job out of graduate school in a multi-modality treatment clinic up in East Harlem. There I got my first formal training – well, informal actually but *real* – in an addiction treatment approach that was really based on a kind of old-school addiction counseling mode that included 12-Step and was based in the disease model. I learned the whole paradigm that we've now come to describe as the "abstinence-only" model. Although I had been trained in a very different way, what I was being taught at the clinic (not that it was necessarily *correct*, mind you) in my entrance into the addiction field was that all of that complex psychological way of thinking was all well and good until it comes to trying to work with people with addiction problems: here's this whole other model that is the only game in town and is the only one that really works. Again, this is what I was being told. So I learned that model somewhat uneasily. And I was left to try to reconcile these two apparently competing points of view.

Over the course of the next seven or eight years, I went on to develop and direct a few addiction treatment programs. I was the Clinical Director of one of the premier intensive outpatient programs in New York at the time. I was still working within this traditional paradigm; this was all in the late 1980s. We had some success and a lot of failure and we came to understand that, within the traditional framework, addiction is a very difficult disease or disorder to treat, that many folks are not ready for sobriety and that we were limited in what we could do – it was just the reality that we had to face up to. That never sat comfortably with me, I have to say, and, as the Clinical Director of this program, I was very interested in looking at outcomes and looking at our success. And over the course of the four years that I directed this program, it began to dawn on me with increasing clarity that we were failing to be of help to the overwhelming majority of the people that initially walked through our doors. It was like a dirty little secret that I was ashamed to admit to myself, let alone to anyone else. I was feeling kind of guilty - and ashamed and anxious and confused - and, ultimately, I came to feel that this was not an acceptable outcome for our treatment program and that the standard treatment model had to be challenged. We were blaming the *patient* for our lack of success rather than becoming curious about what might be wrong with the model and/or the treatment approach.

At this same time, I had the good fortune to start a private practice. In my private practice, I started getting calls from people who were actively using drugs and alcohol and who wanted therapy, but who were not necessarily clear about what they wanted to do about their drug use, or were certainly not ready to stop. Since they seemed to be good therapy candidates, I thought I would become more flexible and sort of see if I could work with them while they were actively using. I began to experiment with a kind of new approach that I think harkened back to my early training and to my continuing experiences of training and therapy and, lo and behold, many of the patients actually stayed in therapy. They were able to meaningfully engage; they began to address their drug use and their drug use began to reduce or in some cases stop; my clinical experience just didn't fit with either the model that I had been taught back in East Harlem or at my then-current well-respected clinic. So these two experiences: 1) the failures of my treatment program and 2) my being able to be helpful to people who weren't supposed to be treatable made it increasingly clear to me that there was another way.

I happened to have a relationship with Alan Marlatt (this was in about 1992), and I remember having a telephone conversation with him - me in New York and he in Seattle - and I said, "Alan, I'm having these treatment experiences with patients that I'm not supposed to be having: people are actually getting better in therapy!" And he said, "You're doing harm reduction work." I had never heard the term before. That was my introduction to the concept of harm reduction. Then Alan began to describe this concept as a kind of alternate paradigm, and it was as if the clouds parted and the sunlight shone through; suddenly everything began to make sense! It seemed to me that this new paradigm explained the failure of the traditional model and also explained why I was having success with my so-called untreatable patients. So, in 1992, my career took a 180 degree turn because harm reduction seemed to offer so much of value and benefit to everything that has to do with both understanding and being helpful to people struggling with addictions or having problems with substance use.

How I've come to understand harm reduction since then is that there's a philosophy that's embodied in harm reduction that we first learned about culturally through needle exchange. And this philosophy has certain fundamental principles that the handful of us who have been working as harm reduction psychotherapists have been applying in psychotherapy. These principles, I think, can be applied in different applications for different clinical populations. Essentially what they have to do with is really radical abandonment of a preconceived idea about who the client is, what the nature of the client's problem is, what the client needs from you, and what you can offer that can be of help to that client. We're challenged to put all of our own preconceptions aside and try to really understand what this person needs and wants and how we can be of help. It completely turns that traditional addiction treatment relationship on its head. Instead of coming in with a whole model about the nature of the addictive disease and what people need to do and the only way they can recover, we actually have to come in open and without seeing that kind of preconceived perspective of people as a kind of countertransference [Editor's note: *countertransference* refers to a therapist's feelings about a client that originate from the therapist's own life experiences and issues] block that prevents us from being able to actually listen to patients.

What that suggests is that we need to listen to the patient and start from where the patient is motivated to seek help, which becomes the starting point of the treatment. And *listening* is the glue that strengthens or facilitates a strong therapeutic alliance, which is crucial in good treatment. Within that therapeutic alliance, we can then develop a collaborative relationship with people around the questions of what hurts, what's harmful, what's not working, what's problematic and how they can begin to set meaningful personal goals in the direction of reducing what hurts or what's harmful, and move in a more positive direction. This is the basis for the whole idea of small, incremental change: steps in the right direction. And what we see is that as people begin to reverse the negative spiral of addiction or problematic substance use and begin to make positive changes, a positive process of change gets set in motion. Small changes lead to other small changes as people begin to feel a little bit better. They feel more empowered and emboldened to take further steps in their lives, more confident about being able to change: like a wheel in motion, this change process gains momentum with each success.

As people begin to feel better, part of what's fueling problematic substance abuse gets taken out of the equation and people's relationship to the substance changes. They may now feel more conflicted about using in problematic ways. They're more motivated to reduce their use or use in a safer way or to stop. They're now increasingly seeing that the important things in their lives, or values, are now being threatened by excessive use. It's about helping people to see more clearly what's happening in their lives. If we think about the safe space of a harm reduction therapeutic context in which the therapist is non-judgmental, compassionate, accepting of all of the aspects of the person, we're now inviting all of those aspects - their substance use, their reasons for using, their other interests in life, their aspirations that have been thwarted, their interest in health and growth – to fully come into the room, and now we can create a context that helps the individual grapple with the potential conflict or problems that their substance use may pose for their pursuit of these other interests. So now it would be possible to talk with people from the *full* experience of who they are, about whether, just maybe, there are other ways to resolve this ambivalence than continuing to do what they've been doing. It becomes possible, then, to think about new possible creative solutions, ways of resolving what is important to them in their lives including their drug use.

One of the things that continues to draw me to harm reduction is its focus on creativity, both for me and for my patients. And how within that creativity, free and open thinking is nurtured, leading both of us to experience a more positive encounter. I think that this creative thinking is also shown in our goal: to be maximally helpful to everyone who walks in our door. I acknowledge that I have limitations; each therapist does, and our limitations are going to frame to whom we can be helpful. Yet the more flexible, free, creative, and willing to be impacted by, molded by, and shaped by a client or our experience with the client - and draw upon whatever seems like it might be helpful - I think the more possibilities open up for how that therapy actually can be helpful.

This is why I think of myself as practicing integrative harm reduction psychotherapy because I wanted to integrate as much as we possibly can, or need to, into the services we provide. We need to be willing to give advice and make suggestions and talk about skills and strategies that might be valuable or useful to experiment with when that seems to be called for. Or, on the other hand, with some people, I need to be all about exploration and clarification, kind of keeping myself out of the way because that would be experienced by that particular patient as a kind of impingement or threat to their sense of autonomy. Other harm reductionists have a more doctrinaire way of doing harm reduction therapy, which I think runs the risk of becoming just what the old abstinence-only paradigm became: that is, the "'there is only one way of recovering" kind of thinking. Some harm reductionists would say, "well, we're going to be *only* about empowerment and staying out of the client's way, and we're not going to give people what they need even when they're completely out of control and need someone to step in and take charge because they can't right at that moment." An example of this is: what if your client was suddenly having a heart attack? You wouldn't simply stand there and do nothing; that would be both unethical and non-humanistic. With substance abuse or other potentially dangerous behaviors, sometimes we have a similar obligation. The real challenge is to be able to use some combination of intellect and theory and intuition, dialogue, and negotiation to figure out *with the client* how they need for us to be in order for us to be most effective for them at this point in their lives. After all, we are service providers, and so we need to provide the service they want and need. Ultimately, we might need to be going in directions with our patients that we hadn't anticipated before.

Harm reduction, as far as I'm concerned, embodies the key concept of moving in a positive direction. It values health and it values life, which is why, from my perspective, the person who is simply about empowering and destigmatizing the addict is not necessarily practicing real harm reduction - if that client is at risk to die or lose their kids or lose their job, then the therapist has a duty to intervene. When we see some clear and present danger that's being imposed by somebody's behavior, it seems to me a harm reduction framework would suggest that we somehow need to discuss it with our patient or intervene or attempt to engage the person in grappling with their risk in some way; we can't simply ignore the risk.

Along with the values of destigmatizing and empowering is the value of understanding the other side of a client's ambivalence, really understanding the reasons why they might still be using. Let me tell a story that I think will help to illustrate the different movements within harm reduction that I think are trying to co-exist or complement one another somehow. I think part of the struggle we're having is because a lot of folks don't come to harm reduction as I did - through a therapeutic door trying to help move clients in a positive direction and improve their quality of life or help them identify personal goals. Rather, a lot of people came into harm reduction as activists both to challenge the stigmatization of drug use and drug users that has contributed to inadequate health care for that population and to help us culturally to view the spread of HIV and AIDS and the incarceration of drug users as prejudicial. So a) these folks don't have clinical training and b) they have a different mission in a sense. Part of their job is to get "'the man" off the drug users' backs. I think most of us agree with this part of our job, but I don't necessarily understand how that part of our job needs to be integrated with this other clinical agenda. So here's the story:

I was supervising someone - this would be around the early 1990s I believe – a social worker, pretty well respected and working in a harm reduction center. He walked into the Day Room one day and Jose, a patient, was lying on a bench nodded out. The social worker looked at Jose and thought that he didn't look very well. So he went up to the caseworker and said, "Hey, what's up with Jose, he doesn't look well." The caseworker said, "Oh, Jose comes in every day; he just gets high and nods out. It's kind of a safe space for him to chill. You know, just leave him alone; don't mess up his high." So the social worker said, "Hmm, okay, but he doesn't really seem to be breathing very well. Have you checked in with him?" At this point, a few of the caseworkers started to get a little angry and said to the social worker, "Look, we know Jose and we're telling you, just leave him alone. He comes in here everyday and this is just his safe space!" The social worker then started to get increasingly anxious. So he went up to Jose and bent down to listen to his breathing to see what was going on, and he noticed that Jose's skin was pale. He thought to himself, "This man is overdosing!" And then said to everyone, "I think this guy is in serious critical condition. Would somebody call 911?" And the caseworkers started yelling at him to back off, so he went and called 911. The EMTs arrived in five or ten minutes and said if they had not arrived for another five or ten minutes, Jose would have been dead. So, here's the punch line: who was practicing harm reduction in this scenario? I think they both were, but they need to find a way to live together - and certainly work together better - for the sake of the well-being of the patient. This story is important to me because it showcases how we're dealing with these broad, diverse groups of people who need different things – whether we're talking about patients or therapists! So, from my point of view, harm reduction means adapting to meet the needs of different people.

Harm reduction psychotherapy also requires that we be both very skillful and very knowledgeable, which is one of the major shortcomings in the traditional drug and alcohol treatment field. And I should say this is true in the original harm reduction grassroots field as well. It is really a reflection of the stigmatization of drug users. That is, in this society we have decided that drug users, whether in harm reduction or traditional drug treatment, don't need sophisticated help. They can benefit from untrained or poorly trained or para-professionally trained folks who have limited education, who care more than anybody and yet are generally quite limited in their knowledge and level of skill.

Instead, I think we're arguing for, as harm reduction psychotherapists, the gold standard: harm reduction psychotherapists need to be highly skilled *and* highly educated *and* highly sophisticated *and* care more than anybody in order to bridge substance use issues with mental health issues along with the biopsychosocial issues that drug use reflects or is entwined with. So, we're really arguing for elevating the entire field in a way.

Now, let me also say that I honor the tradition of self-help in AA and other 12-Step programs, of the therapeutic community movement, and of the grassroots harm reduction movement. All these movements evolved to meet the needs of people who were abandoned by the medical and psychiatric communities along with the rest of society. There's something heroic and tremendously admirable about people stepping up to try to find ways to help one another to make up for this gap. But, then, as history moves on and now we have a whole treatment industry that is founded on being able to hire - to exploit - these folks and pay them poorly and train them poorly, now we've got an industry that has an investment in keeping things the way they are rather than upgrading the level of expectation and skill of these workers because it's going to hurt the industry owners in their pocketbooks. All those certified alcohol counselors make their livelihoods on these jobs, so this change in the field must be a gradual process that respects these realities while still fighting for the gold standard in treatment providers' skills. As with our clients, we need to bring many things to the treatment table including respect, with grassroots spirit and good clinical training skills, to assist clients in seeking their best life possible – their own "gold standard" if you will. Then we will really be practicing harm reduction psychotherapy.

Andrew Tatarsky is in private practice in New York City. He can be reached through his website at www.andrewtatarsky.com.

ALLAN CLEAR

12-STEPPING HARM REDUCTIONIST

I moved to this country from England in about 1982, and I've used drugs since I was a teen. While I was living in New York from 1982 to 1987, I was doing a lot of coke. I was working in a drug bar - I was a bartender in New York – and folks *I* knew started to die of AIDS around 1984-85 (but it wasn't like the horror of the late 80s). In 1987, I quit drugs and went to AA meetings and switched from working in sleazy drug bars to higher-end restaurants. At that time, the mid-to-late 1980s, if you went to AA meetings in the Village, every other person would say, "I have three months at the most to live," and it was literally every other person. Everyone had AIDS. So, I began to be really affected by hearing this all the time – almost like it could've been me saying this because of *my* drug use.

I was often the only straight waiter in the restaurants where I worked. Most of the waiters had HIV. In 1992, in the last restaurant in which I worked, there was a whole wall of lockers, many more lockers than waiters, and a waiter asked someone why there were so many lockers with locks on. They were told it was because the waiters were dead. So, there was one set of people I was with who were dying of AIDS through drug and/or sex stuff and then, at work, there was another set going through the same thing. In 1989, one of the waiters I knew was involved in ACT-UP [Editor's note: Since about 1988, ACT UP has been a diverse, non-partisan group of individuals united in anger and committed to direct action to end the AIDS crisis. See www.actupny.org for more], and I really liked what they were doing, and I wondered what I could be doing. I really liked what they were doing around outreach (i.e., the punk scene in '76 & '77) and other stuff. There was an AA meeting I was at where Rich Delavich was talking (he had been arrested in NYC for doing needle exchange —NE – in the 1990s), and he was talking about AIDS and needle exchange in this meeting. And I thought, "well, that's what I should be doing, drug users are my community, so that's a no-brainer!" And so, I got involved in ACT-UP in late '89. Rich had some meetings of needle exchange in late 1990. Because one of the risks of being a foreigner living in this country without citizenship was being deported for moral turpitude and being involved with drugs was considered moral turpitude, I was prepared to do the support work for NE until we sorted out whether an arrest was imminent and I'd get deported. I stopped doing NE in the fall of 1990 although I actually was arrested by mistake for doing civil disobedience in Atlanta. But I wasn't deported although I could have been for that or for drugs or something else.

I had friends in England who were in recovery, and a lot of people I knew in NE were in recovery. It's odd, sort of, now that it's been over 20 years of sobriety (Oct. 13), but I haven't been to meetings in a really long time. I don't know how others would categorize themselves now (either in recovery or not) but, either way, it's our history, you know, that's how I got where I am now! And I really thought that doing NE was a way to get others into recovery. I really thought that this would begin an entrance into traditional recovery for them. What I discovered was that this, NE or harm reduction, was a means in and of itself for some. I mean I really saw my role as bridging the gap between NE and recovery through my experience in recovery. And I was wrong.

For instance, I would take people to meetings and they wouldn't stay. I would walk them to the door and they wouldn't go in. So, I realized that I needed to change my focus; this gift I have to give other people. On the other hand, I was right. After working in NE for years and years, I saw so many people use NE as a vehicle to get into recovery. But it wasn't *me* that did it. So, I was wrong about *me* being the catalyst that helped people enter recovery, but I was right that NE and harm reduction, and having that as an avenue for people to engage in their circle, did help people get to recovery.

Coming to Harm Reduction Kicking & Screaming

At some point, it became harder and harder to go back to meetings for me, to listen to people whining about going to the dentist when the people I was working with had many more serious issues than that. It became nearly impossible to hear the similarities anymore. In a sense, I found myself being judgmental about it. I wasn't enjoying going to meetings as much. I knew those people had to say the things they were saying, that's what recovery is all about. To me, though, the 12 Steps are a bridge *back* to life, not "a" life but "to" life. I think for some people, AA *becomes* their life and they have to go to meetings five times a day. And for some people who have never known a life, perhaps that's what they need to do.

But in my life, I've done some other things: NE, ACT-UP, photojournalism, but the most radical thing I ever did was recovery because it turned my whole life upside down. And I think, being English, where mental health care – therapy - was not existent, in a room full of people talking about the same stuff, was radical! I remember the image at the time being kind of like my life was black and white and then totally turned to color in recovery. For me, there are so many similarities between harm reduction and 12-Step that when I started doing NE, when I started going to NE conferences and such, most of the folks there would've said they were in recovery. You don't see that as much anymore. In the larger cities - NYC, Chicago, San Francisco - people who are working in NE don't necessarily identify that way now. So, many people in the early history of NE and harm reduction were 12-Step people. One of things that has always bugged me is that the opposition paints harm reduction as enabling people to continue to use. And it just pisses me off. I mean I would sit in meetings and hear about the suffering of people from drugs. All these people who had suffered – why would we want others to suffer, too? We'd have to be a bunch of sadists or something to want that. It's pretty insulting.

It's been my experience, when we were doing NE, moving from underground to overground, that it seemed that a lot of the people doing NE were gay and lesbian activists who didn't have any experience with drug use. So, I felt we needed more people doing this who were in recovery. And, again, I was wrong because people brought their own issues to this work. And you could tell the people who were actually wobbly in their own recoveries because they were so strident about it, preaching it. Dogma is not what this recovery work is about. So, people being in traditional recovery and working in NE actually changed the dynamics of the work. Ironically, it seemed that people who never used drugs were actually less judgmental than those in recovery! I guess because when you are in recovery you have an answer, a solution. And you feel so strongly about that answer – *your* answer- that you want to share it with everyone. So, in the end we had a mix of people. There have always been people in recovery doing this work but they've become quieter.

So, what is recovery? To me personally, recovery is about using the principles I learned in the rooms combined with everything else I've learned. I don't know...it's difficult. I'm not in recovery and yet I *am* in recovery. I wouldn't call myself recovered, though. But I find myself remembering to do things that I learned in the beginning of my recovery, like making amends right there and then. That comes back to me when I haven't done it. And I miss the openness I had in the rooms that I don't have as much now, talking about how I feel.

But I still don't drink and I don't do drugs. I do *think* about doing them but what I have now is much too valuable to give up. To do alcohol and drugs just doesn't seem worthwhile. It would potentially put everything I have now at risk; well, maybe it wouldn't really but it has the potential. It's just not worth it. I'm actually okay with my glass of water or whatever. But, you know, I still like drug users. Drug users are people who like to travel; they love adventure and transformation; they're risk-takers.

You know, I've learned in recovery that you deal with the present and you put it in perspective. No matter what it is, you can say, "well, I lived through this other hell (using) over here; if I can do that, then I can certainly get through this right now." That's the attitude of being in recovery. I can show up for myself, for my family... and for everyone else. I *do* have a choice and I'm choosing to stick with this.

Allan Clear is the Executive Director of the Harm Reduction Coalition in New York City. He can be reached through their website at www.hrc.org.

ANNIE FAHY

12-STEPPING HARM REDUCTIONIST

I worked in traditional alcohol and other drugs treatment in the 1980s and 90s. I was a nurse, and I had trained to be a labor and delivery nurse and a family care nurse. I did home births on the side as well as labor and delivery nursing, and there was a big lawsuit - a hospital case - that split everybody apart at the hospital where I was working. The doctors blamed the nurses and the nurses blamed the doctors. Everybody who had insurance got named, and everyone got deposed. I just really got disillusioned and thought, "I have to get out of here!" I was going to work every day and saw some folks playing volleyball behind the hospital in this treatment center. I thought, "I'll go play volleyball and look; just see what they're doing over there." And I left the hospital and went to work at the treatment center.

I liked the work there (it was a lot like labor and delivery). I found myself sitting with people in a different kind of pain but still in pain, and I was helping them believe that they were going to get something good out of it, just like birth. I also discovered that I was very good at this work, but I was still "just" a nurse; and if you are a nurse in treatment, staff doesn't really want you in the counseling room. So, I ingratiated myself with the staff at the treatment center and discovered that what I had to do in order to "get in" was to offer to deal with the clients that no one else wanted to deal with. And that I did gladly!

The treatment facility was a traditional, insurance-based treatment center. Like most facilities at that time, we would get guys in that we called "frequent flyers:" those male clients who would make several trips to treatment for various reasons, as well as female clients who seemed to leave treatment one day and turn right around, after getting a boyfriend and winding up drunk or using cocaine, and return. I was always up to working with these clients, and I really acquired some good counseling skills that way. I worked on weekends only at this point and even ran some groups after awhile. I then moved into the mental health sector and was working in and ran the group for mandated clients because no one wanted to work with them. I also started a Women's Group. When Welfare Reform came about in 1996 or '97, we got a lot of money to set up women's treatment with kids – both residential and outpatient treatment - and because I had the nursing background as well as a background working with women, the center said, "Do you want to do it?" and of course I said, "Sure!" It was the best job I ever hated.

I loved the work. This was the first time we set up gender-specific treatment. First of all, no one wanted to work with these clients because they were so much work. They were chaotic and illiterate, and they had been getting welfare for a long time so it was difficult to change that culture. Partly this was because their image was that they had become dependent on the welfare system and couldn't get off it. They had a lot of stigma around them, but frankly, I had more trouble with the staff than the clients! The staff was so angry with the clients all the time and took it out on them, and here I was trying to create a non-oppressive treatment program. This is when I really began to appreciate just how oppressive we really were in standard AOD (alcohol and other drugs) treatment in 1988, how bossy with clients. I learned a lot about alcohol and other drugs during these years, but still, that knowledge wasn't enough to help me with my own alcohol trouble that I began to have in the early 1990s.

I had been pretending at work that everything was OK for some time when, really, I was drinking at home - very much wearing a mask. In 1993 I hit my own bottom with alcohol, went to treatment and started my own recovery. So here I was doing all this early recovery work and getting this Women's Program going, and struggling with training staff including this training in Motivational Interviewing that had nothing to do with the book (by the same name)! We got all this gender-specific treatment information together about how to work with women and domestic violence and more, and it had nothing to do with what someone needed in a single day. We would get this information from various people about trauma, but none of it really addressed how to work with a woman's trauma or how to create safety.

During this time, my own life was so chaotic that I would be literally standing on the street corner waiting for a woman and her kid to get off the bus and my cell phone would ring and it would be my own daughter going, "Mom, you were supposed to pick me up from school!" I felt like I never could leave work, like we constantly had a pregnant person who was going to deliver at any minute. The parenting skills that the women had were so different; there were so many complicated cultural issues and black/white issues. It was unbelievable. It was very complicated, and I'm just not an administrator. But I am the best counselor you'd ever want to see, and I can really knock you dead with it, but I had a hard time doing the administrative piece, and I really did have the whole ball of wax on my shoulders. I understood the funding and the money and about two years after we got going - and we were successful - I did some marketing in the community in new ways: I had art projects and all sorts of creative collaborations. We built a playground and other similar projects like that but about two years in, the money person at the agency realized this project generated a lot of money and, if they had a director who didn't know where that money was at all times, they could do a lot more with the money – in other words, they could strip the Women's Program and use that money in other areas of the treatment center. So our program began to be cut. I was pretty burned out, so I decided that I was going to leave the field, leave treatment and do something else.

Right around this time, I went to a training with Edith Springer though I don't think Edith was actually at that training. I think Terry Ruefli came. He was a partner of hers who worked in harm reduction in New York City. So he came and he did the training for Edith: referenced her, put her up on a pedestal, used her words - really channeled her. Everybody in the whole training-- and it was all mental health people-- was a-gasp and I knew this idea – this *harm reduction* - could save me because at its core was this humanity. I knew that this was something that I had been looking for, that I had been trying to get my staff to consider. However, there were aspects about it that were also challenging for me: all this stuff about working with active users and having staff that was still using.

I came from that discipline that said you had to have two years without using before working in the field, although I didn't quite have it when I got back from treatment, and I got drafted back to work in public health because people said, "Oh, you're a good AA member; it's OK!" But frankly, I also knew that I was already working with active users - they just didn't tell me about their use.

We created a lot of liars with those policies, the approach we took in our work. In that training, and in subsequent trainings with Patt Denning and Jeannie Little, I started to get really uncomfortable with my approach, and I started to feel like maybe I don't even know what I'm doing because I started to feel that I was just handing out gold stars to the people that do what I want them to do, and, to everybody else, I'm labeling them. I remember I was in the staff room and people were talking about a woman who was prostituting and using drugs who had come into the detox that we ran to get folks off the streets. It was cold and she was tired and wanted to rest, and everybody was mad at her because she didn't want to stop drinking and she didn't want treatment. She was just being more honest about her goals, and the whole room made fun of her and were really cruel about her sexual life. Then somebody said, "She ain't about nothing," and it broke my heart. I told them I couldn't listen to such talk anymore and how awful they were for saying such things about a client. And then I thought, "I can't work in traditional treatment anymore." Harm reduction had ruined me, but I still didn't want this woman to be using. I was completely confused: I didn't want to support this woman's using, but I also didn't know what else to do. When I spoke up for her in that meeting, though, I became really aware of how lonely it is to speak up for a client that everyone wants to trash and how lonely it is to try to *not* have all the answers and just say I don't know if I'm helping. It seemed like we were giving this woman a break and that might be helpful in keeping her alive. I could tell that what I was saying was radical - even to myself - and it was really lonely. It was this feeling of taking a step into the unknown, not knowing what I'm stepping into. This was very different from traditional treatment where, with the solidity of AA and 12-Step, you really know where you're going and have this sense that this works; that if a client just does it this certain way, then everything will turn out great.

And that's how I came to harm reduction. It just made so much sense that I couldn't deny, and I hadn't been formally trained at that time. I had a certification in addiction counseling that I got through hours of experience and I got lots of CEU's [Editor's note: continuing education units], but I never had any formal education around counseling in my nursing education. I think that after that initial harm reduction training I realized that I had a theoretical framework that was OK for one client and that I didn't have one for another client - and that that was okay. I really kind of made peace with that. Today, I look at it this way: harm reduction is a tool that I use with some people and I may not use it with everybody; I may use a 12-step modality or disease concept, and I think that opens up a lot of thinking about trying different things with different clients and that is really energizing. One thing about me is if I'm energized about something I'm going to want to keep doing it. And I really wanted to keep doing this work.

I was getting a lot from this new way of doing things so I wanted to keep doing it. I felt less and less comfortable in my own 12-Step meetings, though. I had more difficulty with some of the things people said there. The meetings here [Editor's note: Georgia, USA] tend to be pretty churchy. There were things like people being publicly confronted for talking about drugs and not just alcohol. There was a young boy who came into an open meeting once and he was talking about *cutting* [Editor's note: refers to the cutting of one's skin in various areas generally in an attempt to have one's emotional pain shown through this physical manifestation; generally not a suicidal gesture] and not *drinking and cutting*. Some people who thought that topic wasn't appropriate in an AA meeting really slammed him. And the way it happened was just how these kinds of things are often done. I could see the entire meeting take care of this so-called problem: one guy said something and then another guy said something and then others chimed in. It really hurt to watch this young man's vulnerability. I remember thinking, "Bill Wilson would not have done that. Bill Wilson would be turning over in his grave." Someone was coming into this meeting saying that they didn't drink today and that was different for them, and they were talking about how difficult it was not to drink. Isn't that what AA and 12-Step is all about?

I was also running into a lot of clients at meetings, and I was feeling a lot of pressure from 12-Step to be of service. I was beginning to realize that I couldn't sponsor people anymore; it was too difficult with my work. Clients always wanted me to sponsor them. In this town especially a lot of people say, "I haven't seen you around lately," and it's this sideways "got ya!" I could feel myself drifting away from meetings and AA. Not drifting away at all from the principles or the practices or the framework. I was just feeling like I didn't fit there anymore, and it is a lot of work to do my job and be there. Right around that same time was when I got into the Motivational Interviewing training with Bill Miller, who is an incredibly spiritual person – rather like the AA principles come alive. He is just so close to whatever that energy would be that really he just channels love and connection to principles. Around this time, I started to make a real connection with harm reduction. I would see people who I thought were really grounded, but there was also a lot of chaos. I went to the harm reduction conference in Seattle [Editor's Note: 2002] and I was sort of scared there - and I have a high tolerance for people. It was so intense to be at that level of really a new definition of recovery or *recoveries:* the idea of a culture of drug use and people organizing places where they could use dope. Holy smokes. I loved it!

I was worried I would never fit in with my traditional counselor upbringing again. MI, like harm reduction, gave me a place where I could use those traditional skills and also use the spirit of AA – and more. The spirit helped to organize me around my own harm reduction practice. I was also doing a lot of narrative therapy at the time and that's a perfect compliment to MI. And it's all harm reduction.

And that's how I define harm reduction, and I just keep it really simple – *reduce harm*. One of my goals in working with a client is to always look for ways to be helpful, ways to reduce harm and risk to that client, or to help clients identify ways to be safer in whatever they're doing. In that definition I say that, "behavior is just behavior," there aren't some behaviors that are worse than other behaviors, and I really try to practice that in my interactions with people. When I'm working with behavior, it's just the feedback from that person that needs some attention, that's asking me to pay attention. And that's the way I think of harm reduction.

Annie Fahy is a counselor with the Harm Reduction Therapy Center in San Francisco and a Motivational Interviewing trainer in the Bay Area. She can be reached at anniefahy@gmail.com.

MARK KINZLY

12-STEPPING HARM REDUCTIONIST

My story with harm reduction begins with me. I went to treatment 28 times. I think that many people think folks go to treatment to get clean. Not me! I went to reduce my habit and to get people off my back, definitely not to get clean. And you know, strangely, there was nothing different about the first time I went to treatment compared to the 28th time.

I have a 26-year-old daughter, and when she was 10, she said she would no longer come to see me "through Plexiglas." You know, that comment affected me so deeply I couldn't do this any more - use. And gratefully my six-year-old has never had to see me the way my older daughter did. It has been a wonderful experience! I even have a two-year-old grandchild now. My life is so different. Even my daughter's mother was in my last wedding. She did an incredible job throughout my chaotic drug use.

I attend 12-Step meetings now, and they are very beneficial to me, but I am also not someone who disregards the three spiritual principles that we talk about in the fellowships – honesty, open-mindedness, and willingness. The one problem that I have with people who are so staunch and rigid in 12-Step is how they will say that one of the principles is open-mindedness as long as it goes along with what they believe. That's really dangerous, because there are a lot of folks that will never get clean and never stop using. Just as human beings, we should keep them as safe as we possibly can so that maybe, at some point, they will hear the message and might be willing to stop using. I just don't know what it takes for people to stop using, only for myself.

In 1990, I was selling shoes for a major footwear company. I couldn't stay clean though I'd been trying since 1986. I mean really trying since then, and I'd managed to put together 30-60-90 days in a row but couldn't grasp the concept really of how to stay clean. In 1990, I noticed all my friends around me were dying of HIV. It hit me: "this is enough, I can't do it anymore." I ended up getting fired from this shoe company job and started to volunteer at the New Haven Needle Exchange program handing out needles. A brother by the name of George Edwards, a former Black Panther, said to me, "What's the difference between you and the brothers dying around you?" And the answer was that we realized we had access to clean needles. That was the point at which I fully swallowed harm reduction.

There's been a huge transition in the drug culture and treatment world in many ways, mostly due to HIV. I've watched many people get services, some of whom have gotten clean and stayed clean through the needle exchange programs (NEPs). You know, NEPs gave users a place where they felt like they were wanted in a world where they/we always had to hide. I started seeing people in meetings talk about how they were turning their lives around, and this wasn't only about reducing the transmission of a virus, but also connecting people to life-saving information that they might not have or get from somewhere else. You know, I believe that a harm reduction approach works for some folks - not for everyone - in regards to drug use. The point is that we need to have as many "tools on the tool belt" for folks when we are dealing with the different personalities that we deal with. What works for someone else may not work for the next person. We need to have as much information as we can have so that we can utilize that stuff for the people we serve.

There are so many different reasons why people use drugs. A woman comes into my office, getting the shit kicked out of her, three kids at home and has to go home, but she also has to be under the influence to tolerate her life right now. To say to her, "if you stop using, things will get better" is bullshit! We set people up to kill them. Edie Springer said to me, "Mark, when someone comes into your office, instead of taking that negative thing that we deem to be so destructive, the drug, why don't we take something that's a positive thing in their life, that they may actually see as a negative thing, and start there?" That changed my whole idea. Now when folks walk into my office I ask someone, "tell me what you have to do in the course of the day to get your hustle on?" And if they say, "I'm in the sex industry and I have to go out and sell myself," I say,"what an incredible marketing talent you have" and take things from that point. People look at that as being a scumbag. Hey, I disagree. I admire her survival skills – that positive thing that Edie was talking about – and we'll go from that point. All I can say is that when I began to integrate that more positive approach with folks, I started to see greater positive results. So now, when folks we serve come in for housing for instance, instead of saying, "you stop using and we'll get you housing," we say, "we'll get you housing today regardless of whether you stop using" because we know it's more likely they will stop if they're housed!

 I think housing is the most powerful harm reduction tool we have. I do a number of trainings around successfully housing substance users. Have you ever seen anyone trying to get clean that has to sleep under a bridge? If we stabilize them, then we have a chance to work on the other stuff. You can't do a lot of work with people that are homeless, running from the police, whatever. Unfortunately, for some reason there's been this association that harm reduction means that "everything goes" - bull. If you have people finding syringes or fighting in your programs including housing, well, kick them out. But don't kick people out just because they use. That's why they're in there in the first place if they're in treatment! I think that a lot of people have that "everything goes" feeling though, of harm reduction being a free-for-all, *letting* people use. Certainly for people in 12-Step fellowships, there's often no room for substance management. Abstinence might be the way for some of us but for others, there could be a different way.

 People go through periods in their lives where their use may be chaotic for whatever reason. One of the Rand studies shows this: they go into treatment and get clean, then 50% went from chaotic use to occasional use; 25% got sober; and 25% went back to chaotic use. Again, some folks go through periods in their lives where their drug use is chaotic, they need help and their coping mechanism is the drug. This works for a little while, but then stops working for them. Well, they simply got their lives together – for whatever reason. It's just for some people that are motivated to stay abstinent, if there are stable structures in place, their chances of staying clean are much greater. I am particularly awestruck by people that get clean and go back to poverty and degradation. Why is it that some people become chippers [Editor's note: go back to using moderately; "chipping away" at their abstinence] and some people become chaotic users? There are many factors. One of the biggest precursors with chaotic users is poverty. You know, when your back is against the entire team, you tend to use. But genetics and environment don't guarantee that anyone will be an addict. Both of my parents are addicts, but my siblings aren't. I do believe that addicts feel deeper than most human beings, and that's why we use. I can see a little kid and start bawling. I struggle with the intensity of my emotions, though now I cry instead of shooting dope.

Today, I coordinate a multi-site study being done around sexual transmissions of HIV amongst drug users. And I'm a research associate at Yale [Editor's note: In late 2008, Mr. Kinzly left Yale to form a consulting practice]. "From jail to Yale," I like to say! I also work with the crack community – that work may be nearest and dearest to my heart. I'm really proud of what little we've done so far in harm reduction and treatment, and in all areas, including medications. I do a lot of work on strategizing with crack communities. It's exciting to work with these communities that at one time had no engagement at all. Those are the little things that keep me motivated.

One of the things that drives me crazy with 12-Step fellowships, though, is that idea that "if you're using you can't be responsible." That makes about as much sense to me as "one hit of crack and you're addicted." One of the things that I learned is that you are indeed responsible when you are using. Let me give you an example: a woman who found out she was pregnant went on methadone. She went to deliver, and a nurse at the hospital found out she was on methadone and called CPS (child protective services). CPS took the kid. What are you talking about?? She was being totally responsible; methadone does not damage a fetus, but heroin can. She made a responsible and healthy decision – while using. And in return, she lost the baby she was trying to save. I heard a great quote the other day: "the greatest hope I ever found was in the eyes of another drug addict." I like that. I think I'll put that on my wall for the next time – and there will be a next time.

Mark Kinzly is a former Associate Researcher at Yale University and currently an independent consultant on the East Coast. He can be reached at markkinzly@yahoo.com.

LOCHLAN MCHALE

12-STEPPING HARM REDUCTIONIST

Let me begin with my definition of harm reduction: to me, it's obvious – *reducing harm*. And when you keep it strictly to that, you can apply harm reduction to everything. Like with cars – using seat belts – or using condoms for safer sex. Really, you can apply it everywhere in life. I just like to keep the definition simple because it seems that the more you try to detail it down, the more people think harm reduction only has to do with sex or with drugs. So keep it raw: it's just reducing harm, and doing that also allows me to think outside the box more - in all areas of life.

    Harm reduction allows your mind just to go, which is how harm reduction came into my personal life as well. What I mean is that sometimes I'll be sitting with someone, and they'll just be talking about what they're doing and I'll say to myself, "wow, that's a great way to reduce harm!" I just store that conversation away in my head and see if maybe it's applicable in my own life, or down the road for a client or friend. Harm reduction just seemed to bleed over into my personal life. The area that I use harm reduction around the most is with my nicotine. I know it's not in the best interest of my health, but I don't want to abstain from it. So I'm always thinking of new ways to apply harm reduction to it whether it be only in the car or only at home or only in the office or what have you. The point is I practice through trial and error reducing the harm.

I was just so fascinated with this concept of harm reduction that I began to think about it all the time. I came from AA - that's where I got sober – and I value what worked for me. But some time later, I decided to get into the counseling profession and, during my interview for the agency where I now work, I was asked, "What do you know about harm reduction?" I had no education or any formal knowledge of harm reduction or any other theoretical concepts; I was just sober with a 12-Step background. I remember thinking to myself, "Harm reduction, harm reduction, what the heck is that?" and saying to them, "I don't really know a thing about it." They just said, "okay," and I got the job! It was then that I began my formal education about harm reduction.

The agency started teaching me about harm reduction: giving me basic information, sending me to trainings and more. I had one supervisor/mentor when I first started who was so harm reduction-based that anytime a staff member discussed abstinence without first talking harm reduction with a client, she would do a full "investigation" with tons of questions for that staff person to make sure it was client-guided counseling that led to the desire for abstinence, not the staff member's own agenda. I respected this so much because she clearly wanted staff to learn to keep their opinions professional and client-guided or away from their work environment. I remember saying to myself again, "Wow! This is so cool!!" This is an agency that works with youth and really understands that many of them are coming from troubled homes - some are even getting in trouble here.

I can really relate to these clients: I had been that little troublemaker kid that you could NOT tell what to do. I'd just say, "f...you" and off I'd go just to show you who's really in charge. So using this harm reduction thing while working with youth was so cool because I wasn't telling them what to do – I was just sitting there, interacting with kids, having a conversation. That whole idea of just having a conversation with someone - and this is how Motivational Interviewing came to me – was amazing! I didn't know what I was doing at first other than just doing what my supervisor suggested! But now I'd say I was doing a little bit of Motivational Interviewing.

One of my co-workers suggested I check out Motivational Interviewing, which I did – and it's incredible! Sure enough, Motivational Interviewing (MI), which is a part of harm reduction, has become the style that I prefer to use with my clients because it's all about letting the client find out where they're at about things in their life: where do they want to be and how they plan to get there. It also looks at the good things in the client's life; it doesn't just focus on the not-so-good things like traditional treatment typically does. It uses the client's own words to build a relationship, to build rapport. Then the client really gets it that you're listening – and actually *hearing* them - not just making things up to scare them, treating them like they're kids (even though they are). Clients come back and say, "hey, this is OK" which leads to them making changes using their own harm reduction practices! It's like this big circle of harm reduction. Anyway, this is what a typical conversation with one of my clients looks like using harm reduction and MI:

- *Me:* *"So you want to reduce harm while you're smoking crack. What do you think?"*
- *Client: "Well I could try this or I could try that."*
- *Me: "Well, which would you like to try?"*
- *Client: "I think I'd like to try this."*
- *Me: "OK, cool!"*

I mean look at that compared to this:

- *Me: "Smoking crack is really bad for you and you shouldn't be doing it because of XYZ!"*

All I'm going to get is an argument after that statement. There's nowhere else for the client to go. I mean, I've asked for the argument really; it's not the client's fault. I've challenged them.

To me, harm reduction is being honest: it's *accepting* something even when we don't agree with what a kid is doing. Using harm reduction is like we're saying to kids that we understand their need to experience life - have fun, grow, and learn; it's how the majority of all people live and learn after all. It's that "learning through personal experience" that seems especially important to many alcoholics and addicts. The friends I've met in AA, and most other people who are using, seem like they all say that they have to learn through hands-on experiences. So, it seems pretty common for folks to need to try a lot of different ways when they're changing behaviors – and that's harm reduction.

When I first heard about harm reduction, I have to admit, my initial opinion was that it was a step towards abstinence, that abstinence was always the goal. And then, as I learned more about harm reduction, I began to see that it was something completely separate. I mean, if somebody *wants* to establish abstinence they can, but I came to realize that harm reduction wasn't always a stepping-stone to that. It wasn't "okay, I'm going to build this rapport with this person and once they see that their way isn't working a whole bunch, BLAMMO - time for abstinence! Go to an AA meeting/NA meeting, *then* you'll be convinced that abstinence is the better way!" Now, I do think there are a lot of good things within abstinence and 12-Step, a lot of great sayings and mantras that help us get through the rough times, and I believe that many people should probably be abstinent. But here's the other thing: you can be abstinent without going to 12-Step or use 12-Step for a while and then stop attending meetings, but that doesn't mean you don't practice 12-Step at all. I don't really go to meetings anymore, but the one saying that really sticks with me is "the alcoholic mind will play tricks on you." That really reminds me that I need to pay attention and remember what it was like, and how I don't want things to be now. One of the things I do practice that I learned in 12-Step to help me keep things raw and real today is that I still consistently hit my knees both morning and night. Like I said before, the bottom line is that I make a *decision* to do something, or not to. Just because someone else has decided to use a more harm reductionistic approach to *their* drinking and using doesn't mean that I should or that I have to. This is one of the ways that I've learned to separate my life from my client's, and that's really important. It's also one of the ways I came to harm reduction.

The thing that really led me to harm reduction - what really changed my thinking about harm reduction - was when I stepped back and realized "wait a minute, I'm seeing clients *completely* switch their lives around and start making these incredible changes through harm reduction, and they're going in a direction they *want* to go without doing abstinence-based stuff." But then, of course, my alcoholic mind starts going "wow, I wonder if *I* could do that?!" Again, to really understand harm reduction, it took me being consistent and saying to myself that "this (abstinence) is what works for me and that (harm reduction) is what works for that person." I know what works for me. I know what I have now for not drinking and drugging, and I know what I had when I was doing it; I don't want to risk that. But that's me and my life, and not my clients – and that's a huge difference.

I do run into clients when I'm at shows and places, and I always go to the back of the stage, or I leave. I don't like to bleed my counseling life with my other life because that's my personal life. I'm a different person in many ways in my personal life than I am at work. For instance, sometimes people see me as a hard ass at work because I enforce the rules. I tell folks that I do that so that they can be safe, and most of them understand that. But in my life outside of work, I'm not all about enforcing rules. I don't want my counseling life to be the same as my personal life. I like to keep the two separate. One of the biggest reasons I do that is because of my music life. If a client knew about that side of my life, they might come after me for only that reason. That's why I've come up with the plans I have for when I'm at shows and run into clients (there are certain clients that show up at a lot of the music venues where I am working). I've talked to them in the counseling room about how that's my personal life and what boundaries I have professionally around that for their safety and for mine. We talked about it and they've come to understand the boundaries, but it can get confusing juggling the many roles! But you know, I love all the things I do and I'm not willing to give them up just because I'm a counselor. Now that's my own life version of harm reduction!

I don't know how else to say it: harm reduction is just that – reducing harm. I hear the struggles going on with other students around harm reduction, and I hear their struggles with clients and say to myself "wow, I don't have those kind of problems with clients." And I think it's the model I use versus what they're using; there's just much less resistance in harm reduction. For instance, the other night one of my peers was saying to the class that she was having a really difficult time with this client who's been at her program four times. She said the client is really reluctant and challenging her. The teacher opened up the conversation to the class and said, "So what do you all think?" I was probably the second or third person to talk and I said, "Well how about thinking outside of the box? This client's been there 3-4 different times. They're back again to this program that's always been very educational: 'you're doing this wrong' (it's a drug diversion program for a DUI). How about letting the client tell you what they're feeling, what they want to do? Use more Motivational Interviewing and harm reductionistic approaches." And she said, "Oh, I can't do that." And I said, "I don't understand. You're serving the *client*, who's been there three or four times!" You could just hear the other students who don't use harm reduction sort of moan and roll their eyes at me, like I just didn't get it and the conversation went totally that way after that. But maybe that's what attracts me to harm reduction – it's outside of the box. It's different, and I like different. It's not doing the same thing over and over again. And after all, if I liked doing the same thing, I wouldn't look like I do or be who I am. And that's harm reduction.

Lochlan McHale is Manager, Haight Street Referral Center & Outreach at Larkin Street Youth Services in San Francisco, CA, and a consultant with UpFront Programs in Crockett, CA. He can be reached at lochlancoffin@yahoo.com.

STEVE M.

12-STEPPING HARM REDUCTIONIST

I first got involved in harm reduction during the nearly eight years I was on methadone. The whole methadone thing was hard for me because the whole time I was on methadone, I was really anti-methadone! Being on methadone always made me feel like I was still using, like I wasn't serious about my recovery. That was the attitude I had about methadone, about *anybody* on methadone; I was still "using."

Because I came from Narcotics Anonymous, the 12-Step program, I had it ingrained in me that if you're taking anything - psych meds or anything - you're not "clean and sober." As a result of that teaching, I made it my goal to get off methadone and to get some drug and alcohol education. I got a job at Walden House as a methadone counselor and began to learn that I couldn't be worried about my needs and wants all the time. I learned that if I wanted to work in this field, I had to learn to be more compassionate and empathetic, and I needed to be able to be patient. I also really needed to learn how to listen to what people say and appreciate and understand what they're feeling as opposed to my thinking that I always know what's best for others. So I started going to school and listening, and I really came to harm reduction by understanding that methadone is a part of harm reduction.

Methadone to me is not an *issue* of recovery; it's a *tool* of recovery. In other words, it was a drug that was helping me to *be* in recovery. When I began to see it in this way, I started seeking out more about methadone. I got books, read articles, talked to people – whatever - in order to get more basic information about methadone: why it's used, what it is, how it helps prevent people from hurting themselves and others. You know, the pros and cons of methadone. Well, I guess I already knew the cons of methadone! So I really focused more on learning about the pros; learning that there really *were* pros to methadone. I began to realize that even if methadone only kept people out of prison or kept them from committing felonies, then it was a useful *medication*. And that was another part of my transformation: I began to see methadone as *medication,* not as a drug only slightly less bad than heroin. That was a huge change in me.

People say that we often change our minds about something because of our own experiences or the experiences of someone close to us. In my case, I can see that I began to shift after my relapse following six years "clean and sober." You know, that relapse made me realize that some of the things that I was doing just weren't working. One of those things was my self-centeredness. I wasn't feeling compassion or empathy for others; I was rigid about what people "could" do, and how you were "supposed" to define recovery. For me, that relapse happened because I wasn't acting in a way that was in keeping with my values. I think of myself as a spiritual person, and I define spirituality as compassion, empathy, patience and willingness - helping people and appreciating what they've experienced. And yet, it was clear that in being so rigid, I wasn't connecting to people, or to myself, in those ways.

For instance, I couldn't see for a long time how great methadone was at helping to keep people from using dirty needles. I just couldn't see it. When I finally opened my eyes, I got to see how methadone was helping prevent HIV and AIDS and also how it helped families come back together, sometimes even those families whose members were really kind of resistant to methadone because they were uneducated – or *miseducated* - about it just like I had been. I mean, methadone is an opiate, okay, and an opiate is a drug. But harm reduction goes beyond that, beyond the superficiality of that statement and says "look at the fact the methadone helps people from going out there and hurting, harming themselves and others." Harm reduction means just that: harm *reduction*!

In the last few years of educating myself, I had become a strong advocate for those on methadone. Now, if somebody comes into my program where I work at Walden House and they're on methadone, I assess them and whatever they choose to do; I'm in their corner as opposed to encouraging them to get off methadone. For instance, let's say I get a 55-year-old guy in who's been on methadone for 20 years and spent 25 years in prison, and the only success he's had is being on methadone. He says he just doesn't know how to stop shooting heroin when he's not on methadone. So I would encourage him to stay on it.

On the other end of that, if a 20-year-old comes in who has only been using heroin for a couple of years and he's talking about being on methadone for the rest of his life, I might encourage him to try not using methadone. But even then a part of me sometimes feels that I'm not doing the right thing. Still, a 20-year-old who has only been using a short time, still has his health, his physical shape - if anybody is going to be able to taper off methadone slowly and successfully, it's someone at a younger age as opposed to an older age. I guess I'm still a little ambivalent about that.

I also took it upon myself to start a 12-Step based Methadone Anonymous group at one of our clinics. It's not getting a lot of support, but I went to a conference in Washington DC, and a gentleman - Fred something – told me he started Methadone Anonymous back East. He said they have about 18 or 19 Methadone Anonymous meetings out there in clinics, and he told me the best place to have a meeting was in clinics because that's where the clients are - they're dosing or seeing the doctor - and the chances of getting the clients to go to a meeting would be greater in a clinic as opposed to an outside place.

Let me tell you just a little about Methadone Anonymous, or MethAnon. MethAnon has its own 12-Step book - and 12 Traditions - although it's a small book. The purpose of MethAnon for me is that it provides a safe place. And like AA, the 1st Step in MethAnon states: "The only requirement for membership is the desire to stop using drugs or alcohol." Members can either stay on methadone or they can be working towards abstinence from methadone - it's up to the member to choose their goal. MethAnon is just a safe place to go for people on methadone where they don't have to feel like if they pick up a chip [Editor's note: "chips" are plastic or metal 'coins' resembling a poker chip – hence the name - that denotes one's time abstinent. Generally these "chips" are marked from 24 hours to unlimited years, and are provided free at 12-Step meetings called *chip meetings*.], they have to give it back because they're not "clean and sober" – they're on methadone. It's just a 12-Step environment for people on methadone, talking about methadone issues. It's a great idea. I mean I've gone to all of the methadone clinics in San Francisco, and I've given them flyers about our MethAnon meeting. I've advocated making it a part of the intake process so when a client comes in, he's handed a flyer about it so he knows there is a 12-Step Methadone Anonymous meeting to go to if he chooses rather than only traditional 12-Step meetings – or in addition to them.

It's a really slow process to get folks to attend. People filter in and some don't stay, but some do stay. We've been doing it about eight or nine weeks now, and we get between two to five people at each meeting. You know what they say about a meeting: "if there are two people in a meeting then it's a meeting." And the methadone clinics are very supportive of it.

So, you can hear, I think, I just keep trying to find ways to mix 12-Step and harm reduction. I mean the first time I heard the term harm reduction, I didn't even think about it. It wasn't until I went to my first training with Jeannie Little that I got the true definition of harm reduction, and it's anything that reduces harm. I've had to go from the philosophy of strictly 12-Step and abstinence to a philosophy of kind of whatever reduces the harm for a client and whatever they're willing to do, too. After all, I can't force anybody to do anything, and I think that's what harm reduction really is all about: realizing that we're not the ones with all the power; it's the clients that have control over their lives. And they're the ones that should. After all, it's their life; I have my own to work on!

Steve is an alcohol and other drugs counselor in the Bay Area. He wishes to remain anonymous.

EDWARD REED

12-STEPPING HARM REDUCTIONIST

My entrance into harm reduction happened some years ago (in 1969) while working as an Addiction Consultant to a County Medical Administrator in the Central Valley of California. I had recommended that the County undertake an addiction rehabilitation project using methadone as a means to traditional abstinence recovery. In the US at the time, methadone was being used for addiction maintenance and, to a lesser extent, for detox from heroin – but that was being done in only one other California county, and it was seen as very controversial. So methadone treatment became my first foray into this world of reducing harm to addicts.

I had gone to New York in 1967 to observe the pioneering work of Drs. Marie Nyswander and Vincent Dole (the husband and wife team who had developed methadone) with opiate addicts, returning with the idea that we could use methadone in our project as an addiction stabilizing agent because we wanted to see if addicts' lives could be normalized using this new medication, as some of us believed they could. The site chosen for our project was one of the State-run mental hospitals that were being phased out by then-Governor Ronald Reagan. They were glad to see us coming and offered to provide the medical staffing - a marriage made in heaven! However, interestingly enough, the psychiatrists in our project, being rather ignorant on the specifics of addiction, were more interested in stepping outside the boundaries of our protocol simply to discover how much methadone a patient would take (this was completely unethical in my opinion). They could have asked any addict in the project to answer that question! I argued against their proposal, as it had nothing to do with the protocol. They also wanted to put people on methadone maintenance but, again, the protocol wasn't written for that.

We had approached the project to learn more about the best practices of addiction stabilization with methadone: to discover if providing addicts with classes in behavioral health and job search skills could facilitate a more normal life for them. Again, the medical staff at the hospital didn't have the same idea. Instead they wanted to discover how much methadone an addict would take in order to seek funding for their imperiled hospital to make it a center for methadone maintenance research, and they felt that this information would help them in this quest.

In all honesty, we might have had a less abortive effort had I myself not been discovered - and gleefully discredited - as a practicing heroin addict. The ironic part of this story is that I had managed to pull off this entire project while in the midst of my own heroin addiction! Further, although I was one of the first clients in this study - the second methadone project in the state - and since I was the last remaining author of the protocol still with the project, it was left to me to supervise methadone dispensing and the record keeping for the project from a room next door. Complete insanity because they did not want to lose the project! I finally blew the whistle to Sacramento about the need for a project audit, and the project was terminated. When we shut that program down, the only choice the study participants had was to jump through bureaucratic hoops to get methadone, and I wasn't good at doing that. I got arrested not too long after that, and the court sent me to Our Family drug treatment program at Napa State Hospital.

Methadone can absolutely help addicts normalize their lives. For that the addict needs education. This is the area in which treatment programs show their ignorance. It is not enough to remove the need for the illicit drug. We have to deal with the fundamental and crippling societal ignorance, to paraphrase the author and renowned Buddhist nun, Pema Chodron. Culturally, America has a Puritanical belief that punishing addicts, or other perpetrators of crime, will cause them to behave better, in spite of a lack of any empirical data showing this to be true and the staggering costs.

Also, I still sometimes wonder about how safe methadone is in the long run. Frankly, I'd rather give people heroin, like they used to do in the UK. I really think if drugs were legal and controlled, especially heroin, it would be better: heroin has few side effects and it is the most effective pain reliever known to man. This wouldn't have worked for me, as I didn't have a stable supply, but had it been legal and controlled, I could see it working - for me and for others. Again, like they did in the UK for years. And I won't even begin to discuss the monstrosity of narcotic illegality, the self-serving origins of our drug laws, and the horrors of the enforcement of those laws in America and in the rest of the world. It is truly time to take a fresh look at the entire subject of drugs in America.

My focus in clinical work has always been about the reduction of morbidity and mortality. That's the phrase I use constantly and that, for me, has to be the goal. Whatever you do, set it up to where people aren't dying because of our insane mistaken attitudes around addiction and the desire by those in power to control those who are addicted. You know, the first time I heard about harm reduction, I thought it was right thinking. And I've been thinking that way ever since.

Ed Reed is a health advocate with Kaiser Permanente in Vallejo, CA. He is also a professional jazz singer. Ed can be reached through www.edreedsings.com.

CHUCK RIES

12-STEPPING HARM REDUCTIONIST

It's almost impossible for me to think about the phrase 'harm reduction' without it having all this baggage attached to it. Just like the word recovery. I think what we're really trying to talk about is the practice of good social work which is meeting people where they're at, helping them to identify what's important to them, and then assisting them in moving in the direction which makes most sense to them. This shouldn't be a political issue. It's really the only way that you can work with anybody to create that alliance. And that alliance has got to be based on mutual respect. Not just respecting the individual but respecting their right to make choices for themselves, whether or not you think they're good ones or bad ones. Harm reduction also believes in helping to support folks to deal with the consequences - the fallout - of those choices, both positive and negative. You know, you do what you do and then you figure out if it's a bad thing or not. For some people traditional recovery is an essential piece of self-care as not everyone is able to maintain a healthy relationship with any sort of drug and alcohol, it's just not possible. So for them, abstinence is absolutely essential.

However, even for those folks, in my experience, probably 90% if not more eventually go back to creating some sort of healthy, balanced relationship with some sort of intoxicant. Most people don't stay sober their whole lives; they learn how to drink or smoke weed or whatever. You could say they go back to using a 'soft drug.'

There are all these theories about soft drugs, too. Some that say if you used any substance chronically over time, there are changes in brain chemistry that don't allow you to go back to that sort of casual control. I don't necessarily know if that's true. I mean I think it's really an individual thing, and I think it really depends on genetics, environment - all sorts of things. I think that there are some people who can't go back, and I think there are other people that can. I think that for some people there are drugs that are really hard to manage. For instance, I see amphetamines are really hard to manage and it seems that cocaine is, too.

Those high intensity stimulants are ones that really require a certain commitment to time and energy and don't really allow people to function all that well while they're on them. Some people can use speed and go to work but my experience is that most don't keep their jobs that long.

For me, recovery was a way to kind of gain a sense - or begin to gain a sense - of who I was as an adult. I don't know about others but I started using when I was young, I started drinking when I was 12. And shooting dope [Editor's note: slang for *heroin*] when I was 14. I just kind of ran from there so I never really had any kind of coherent adult identity, except as a drug user, I mean 'cause that's all I did.

And so again, you go with what you know. So when that identity as a drug user no longer became viable, and what I needed to do to maintain that identity really continued to erode my own sense of values and morals, I knew I just needed to stop. More than anything I just needed to stop and take a break and figure out what the f--k I was doing. It was kind of funny how that all happened. I was 14 – in 1969 - a long time ago.

They didn't have drug treatment then especially not for teenagers. I was getting arrested all the time for stupid things like curfew back when they enforced it or disorderly conduct. Sometimes there would be some dumb drug charge that they couldn't pin on me (I was just a little kid who had long hair and in Chicago at that point you got harassed, everybody did) and so I kept on getting arrested and then they'd release me to my parents. I'd get the ride home with a lecture but my parents were clueless. Finally I got arrested one last time for possession of LSD, for which prosecutors weren't going to press charges *if* my parents did one of two things: put me in an institution or make me leave the state; law enforcement told my folks I was out of control. My stepfather had health insurance and the health insurance covered commitment to a mental hospital. So that's what they did, they committed me. So I go into the hospital and I slept for a couple of days because I was cleaning up and it was very scary. I would always sleep when I went to jail to just deal with the stress but I was feeling better, I was feeling kind of good actually and I sat down with a psychiatrist to do the intake assessment. He gave me the whole range: the blocks and the pictures and everything – the mental status exam. And I kind of liked it. He was asking me things about myself: "What do you think;" "How do you feel?" It was kind of sweet. It felt like he was genuinely interested in what was going on for me, which was something I didn't feel from my family. I really had the desire to be honest about what I was doing, because you *wanna* be honest when you think someone really cares. Even then - even though I was a dope fiend - I thought, "This person is giving me some love so I'm gonna be honest." Now I didn't tell him about my injection drug use because I'm not that stupid but I did tell him about all the rest of the stuff. So it's all over and a couple of weeks later I realize that I could be locked up in this place indefinitely, it's an indefinite commitment. I went to whoever it was and I asked, "Why am I here?" and they said, "Well, you're here because you have behavioral problems at home blah, blah, blah, but mostly you're here because you take drugs. "I take drugs? You didn't even know I took drugs until you brought me in here and I told you!" and they said, "Yeah, but you *did* tell us" and right then I thought, "F--k me! I'll never do that again!" So my honest desire to really just talk about what was really going on for me actually got me locked up. It was horrible; I was as angry as only a self-righteous 14-year-old can be. A couple of weeks later I broke out with some of the others and we went on the run. But you know, I felt so betrayed by that whole experience with the psychiatrist that I made a decision, based in large part on that betrayal, that I was never going to put myself at risk again by telling the truth about my drug use to anyone with any power. And I didn't. I just went underground and become a really good liar. I learned how to 'spin the tale' in a way that you use the smallest amount of lies. You become a kind of lawyer, spinning tales and eventually what that does, especially as a young man, is to teach you that it's not what you do but rather it's what you get away with that counts. It's an interesting bit of a cultural phenomenon. So my friends and I just used everyday from then on. We did a lot of different drugs. We would kind of flow in and out of hardcore drug use. We'd shoot dope for a while and then we'd stop and then we'd be shooting PCP for a while and then we'd stop. It was just this sort of weird ebb and flow thing. We also worked; we weren't criminals. Well, let's say we did criminal stuff all the time but we weren't *professional* criminals - we had jobs, *crummy* jobs!

We had crummy jobs because most of us hadn't finished high school. I only needed another half a year to graduate but there was no way I could do it. I think having been told all that stuff about being incorrigible and out of control did something to me. I came from a very working class family and I was doing all these drugs but there was also this kind of political consciousness that went along with it. I really thank those guys; I really thank them for helping me understand in such a broader way what the realities of the world are/were. They truly believed that there was something to be done to make the world better, to fight the good fight. And they taught me that in spite of how powerful the systems are that you're fighting, you can still successfully —or not - fight them. They organized the masses, that kind of shit. I was the masses but I didn't know that so when I dropped out of high school I went to work in a steel mill; pounded steel all night long actually, the second shift. That was the kind of job my friends and I got. We dropped out of high school but we weren't stupid; we actually read a lot and had this large understanding of the world but school just was not an option. Nobody, *nobody* in my family, or anybody I knew, went to college. We all left and we went to work because work gave us the illusion of independence and adulthood - you got some money.

Well, you got the illusion of being an adult. But you know, throughout all that there was constant drug use and, you know, I was able to totally maintain for a long time. I mean I wasn't really *doing* anything; from about 1975 to 1985 I just went from job to job; I was a f--ked up, working class kind of guy. And then this *thing* happened, which is how I came to Harm Reduction. The last 3 years of my life then had been about finding a woman that would kind of support me. I'd work and do my thing but we'd have that symbiotic relationship where we could both be self destructive in our own way but we'd live together and sleep together, that kind of thing. I don't know what else to call it - it's like a business partnership with a little sex thrown in. I was in San Francisco and I'd been with this woman since 1985. In San Francisco, my heroin addiction really got out of control and that was a real problem because I couldn't afford it. By that time I'd been in and out of methadone programs; it was easy to get in them and with methadone I'd kind of maintain for a while, but I never listened to their mantra of getting clean - it wasn't anything that I really cared about doing. Well, at that time, I lived right up the street from the Haight-Ashbury Free Clinic and they were doing HIV testing. They were paying $8 for the test and $8 for the post-test; it was 1985. They wouldn't give you $10 because they thought you'd go buy dope with it but they would give you $8! So I went in and there's all these sweet graduate student interns looking very attractive. And the men and the women there, they're very attractive and nicely dressed and kind of hip and pretty smart. That impressed me but then they started asking me questions about what I did and why I did it. But no one had really asked me questions like that or in that way - there were no strings attached: I wasn't trying to get drugs from them and they weren't trying to figure out what to do with me, or to make me stop. They were just curious; they wanted to fill out their little forms. But I found that within that dynamic I was able to listen to their questions and honestly reflect on what they were asking and what it meant to me, and then give them honest answers. The most interesting part was that I left the pre-test interview really thinking, "Why *do* I do these things?" It's a really good question, you know? But it had never come up before, and it really rattled my cage. It was a powerful moment. When you have the feeling of safety and trust in the relationship, you're able to hear an outside perspective and reflect on what it means rather than just feeling that you're just stuck in this system, chasing your tail.

So they did this wonderful thing for me and they had no idea they were doing it. And I really started to look at what I was doing and the effect it was having on me, and whether I thought that was a positive effect or not. I began to look at where I envisioned things going in my life, the effect that I had on the world around me, and it really just opened up this whole line of inquiry. You know, I think that many times before I had operated under the illusion that I was an adventurer or an experimenter in the world and I was just trying to find out what life was all about. But self-reflection wasn't really a part of that; it was more of a visceral experience, just a "how-are-you-feeling kind of experience." So I took that away and you know about a year and a half later I decided that I was done using – that was it. And it really was like that; my life had pretty much fallen apart but more importantly, my feelings about what I was doing were so negative and I just felt so bad that I couldn't stop using because there was nothing else to do. There wasn't a compulsive piece to my need to stop but the more I did it, the more I went to the clinic - because I didn't have any place else to go. It was like living a rerun – you know how it ends but you just keep watching. I really credit those folks at the Haight-Ashbury who helped me start that whole treatment/clean-up-my-life process. Because of them, I went into drug treatment, a modified TC (or Therapeutic Community) up in Marin County, and that was on October 14th, 1987 and I have been addiction free ever since.

For me, harm reduction was never really an issue. I started doing syringe exchange in 1989/1990 not long after I got out of drug treatment. Then I started working in drug treatment while staying with the syringe exchange. Even though my motivation back then was different, I really understood that everybody deserves equal access to all possible health care, whether they're using or not. When I first started working in the field, the mantra was: "Keep them HIV negative until they can get clean."

That was harm reduction in its infancy, the whole syringe exchange thing and I was right there with it. I ran these drug programs, homeless shelters, halfway houses and drop-in centers, and back then it was all about abstinence. I'd go and do my syringe exchange thing but when I came back and dealt with our folks, especially regarding housing, it was all about abstinence. Folks weren't being abstinent of course and so we would deny them services and housing based on their inability to quit using. I feel really bad about that now. The way we look at drugs and drug users, and youth, is very punitive; it's all designed to keep the system in place which is the same as any abusive family system -it's always designed with the system in mind first not the individuals. And I came out of that so initially that's where I was for probably the first 8 years I was abstinent. I was heavily into 12-step recovery, medical-model drug treatment and such, and even though I had this harm reduction practice that I did – needle exchange - how I operated in the world and worked in it was just not that way. I credit many people in the harm reduction field who worked hard to open that discussion with folks like me and there are a lot of people like me. I mean there are a lot of people in the field who come from a 12-Step background. And the model that we've come from has been used to hurting people. You know, it has done a lot of damage to a lot of people, and those people are angry about it, rightfully so. It's hard.

You know, I'm a reluctant harm reductionist. I mean I have that personal history and I hated that whole thing and I totally believe in the social justice component as my history would tell you but I'm a pragmatist. I can be a good soldier; I can do the stuff that needs to get done even though I don't really like it, if I see that the end result is worth it. What I can't be is a good German; you know the kind who just goes along even though they see the damage. For many years - when I was working in the abstinence-based world - I felt like I was being a good soldier; I didn't like what I was doing, actually, I hated denying people services; it felt terrible. After a while I started to look around and think, "So, where is the success here?" I saw that most people were leaving treatment still feeling like a failure so what is the point? And of the 10% who leave treatment and still aren't using 2 years later, how many of them go on to have decent, fulfilling lives? Not many. In fact, the percentage was so small that it just seemed like there was something really, really wrong with the entire treatment system. I was lucky enough to be working in a program that gave us a lot of freedom and so we started being less stern with users. We started to talk about having injection drug users groups and we started to learn more about things that not only felt better to us but also got a better reaction from the people we were working with. They weren't necessary 'clean and sober' but they were engaged in the treatment process with us.

What we really noticed was not only was there more opportunity for change but there was also more opportunity for connection and relationship. Change, absolutely but more than that, we could sit down just like I did with those folks at the Haight Ashbury Clinic and have a *conversation.* In fact, this worked so well that when I got the opportunity to create this program at the school I thought, "OK, I can do whatever I want." The school district is a pathetic excuse for any kind of oversight so I'm gonna take that opportunity, and so we created this program that is completely harm reduction-based. And I think in the 8 years we've been there, I've sent 2 people to get treatment; they both absolutely hated it and the only reason that I used classic intervention and forced them into treatment was because they were both so engaged in high-risk dangerous behaviors that the only thing I could see to do was to get them off the street. And treatment got them off the streets.

These kids were involved in just incredibly high-risk behaviors and were very young - 13/14-year-olds, deeply involved in not just drug use but self-destruction. And in that case again you use what you have and drug treatment was the only thing that I had. It was a horrible situation having the huge negative critique I have about drug treatment, especially adolescent drug treatment. It's just a terrible, terrible system and it, just like all drug treatment, fosters and creates the same dynamics that were created in the abusive families that they came from. Exactly the same thing: "F--k you and what you want and need. You do what we think is right," or "This is what's best for the program and you don't need to understand, just do it. And if you don't do it, we'll kick your ass out!" See? No difference. It's shocking! And, up until this year, we were in deep collaboration with a traditional residential drug treatment program in Oakland. We would bring their senior peers over to our program and we'd train them to facilitate groups, and they ran groups with us and for us. So the students at the school loved it and the folks at the treatment program loved it. You might wonder how we got away with this harm reduction approach in collaboration with such a traditional drug treatment program. Well, here's what we would say to the drug treatment staff facilitators: we'd interview them, just like for a job, and we'd say, "We don't want to hear the jargon in groups - not interested. We want to hear what's real in these kids' lives, what they're good at, what you're victorious over and what you're struggling with; that's what we wanna know. We don't wanna hear "One day at a time;" we wouldn't say it in that way. And these kids really liked it and so we did that for 5 solid years; we allowed staff from this traditional drug treatment program to facilitate these harm reduction-based groups with active users with people who were high in the group. Then the student/clients would go back to the drug treatment program, and at the end of every year it'd be like, "Hey, these kids are really catching on!" And I'd go up to the administrators of the school and ask, "So, how you doing?" And I'd hear, "Ah, it's great, wow, what you're doing with our kids, it's great!" And I'd respond with, "Really, so you know what we're doing?" "Oh yeah, yeah," they'd say.

So, there's never been any problem, not with this combination of harm reduction and traditional staff nor with the administrators of the school. They'd all come back from these annual meetings and say they'd had a wonderful time that they felt good about what we were doing. They'd say that the work felt important to them that they liked that they were being of service to these kids. And they'd say that "the rest" didn't matter.

It was within these conversations that I began to realize that in spite of the over- arching philosophy and practice that many people who work at the school program, and have worked there for a long time, absolutely say, "This is a harm reduction program because it has to be." It has to be because if all our young people go out and use, and they all do, then what the hell else are we going to do? We are certainly not going to be an abstinence-focused program 'cause that doesn't work.

You know though, at the school we really believe that sort of practice is not even harm reduction but rather it's just good social work practice. And it will not only work anywhere but if you start it up, it will take hold and grow on it's own. It feeds itself because it's that kind of program. It's not a closed system like drug treatment, it's sustainable and people come and use it and then give back so it's very much a grassroots-organized thing. My experience with the traditional drug treatment program is just an example of that. You know, I think that harm reduction or no harm reduction, I just want to see the work done well. My drive is to create programs that are sustainable and that are run by folks who are really good at what they do and are able to be with young people in a way that is honest and genuine, and that allows young people to be honest and genuine in return. From that, everything is possible. Like I said in the beginning - I'm a pragmatist and I do this 'cause it works. But if it stopped working, I'd do something else.

Chuck Ries is the Director of UpFront Programs in Oakland, CA. He can be reached at chuckries@upfrontprograms.org. For more on UpFront school programs, go to www.upfrontprograms.com.

PAM SMITHSTAN

12-STEPPING HARM REDUCTIONIST

When I think of harm reduction, the first thing I think of is how sad it is that in all the addictions classes I took, they never taught me anything about harm reduction. I would have to learn about that concept from other people and places. And one of those people came to me in 1994. At that time, I got a contract with Sacramento (CA) County to write the curriculum for some four-day addiction classes I was also to teach, which I've now been doing for 14 years. Toni Moore, the lead on this project, said, "You *will* incorporate harm reduction and methadone in this curriculum!" I was working with someone else on this project (we were both 12-Steppers) and when Toni would leave the room, we would look at each other and say, "Whatever! We're *not* doing that. That's a ridiculous idea!" But you know, Toni was absolutely right to insist that we include information on harm reduction because people working with people with addictions needed to know accurate information about harm reduction. It took me a while to learn just how right she was, though!

When I finally became aware of harm reduction – *real* harm reduction – it was after watching an ABC News Special: "America's War on Drugs: Searching for Solutions" (1995) with Catherine Crier. It blew my mind. It included interviews with people like Judge Mike Gray and Kurt Schmoke (ex-Mayor of Baltimore, Maryland) talking about how the drug war was behind so many of the social ills we were having in the US. And then I began to read books like *Drug Crazy* (1998) by Judge Mike Gray and *Reckoning: Drugs, the Cities, and The American Future* by Elliott Currie (1994). I was very lucky that my drug using days never ended up with me in the criminal justice system, and I do, in part, attribute that to being raised in a middle-class neighborhood and being white and female: I just don't fit the typical drug user/dealer demographics. These were the things that began to get me thinking differently about harm reduction and how I, and we as a nation, looked at drug use in general.

When I started writing that addictions curriculum in 1994, I felt that, since I was a recovering addict and alcoholic, that gave me knowledge about addictions, and with a master's degree on top of that, I had everything I needed to both write this curriculum and teach it. I was so wrong! First of all, I know 20 times more now about addiction than I did then. My view then was so much more limited. As a result of my continued education, those addiction classes have changed a lot over the years. One of the biggest ways they have changed has been due to research on methadone: for instance, according to the CalData study in 1994, for every dollar invested in methadone, twelve dollars is returned in savings to the community.

I had somebody in class not too long ago who went home and talked to a friend of hers about harm reduction after that evening's lecture. Apparently, she and her friend got in a heated argument about harm reduction because her friend was in AA and said that harm reduction was against AA principles. I told my student that I used to be just like her friend: extremely closed-minded. We talked for a while about my experience of being so close-minded and the arrogance I felt I had shown to others as a result of that thinking. She seemed to find our talk helpful, but she was still upset about her friend's reaction. I hear stories like these quite often, both the person struggling to see the benefits of harm reduction and the 12-Stepper struggling against it because a premise of 12-Step programs is that alcoholics and addicts *cannot* control their use of substances. I sometimes think of my work today as an "amends," to use 12-Step language, for all the times I loudly and forcefully spoke up - without knowing what I was talking about - about the harms of harm reduction. I really did sound like the ignorant smart aleck I was. And I thought I was so smart back then!

I see harm reduction as a continuum of possibilities, of modifications that someone can make in their life that would potentially reduce harm to themselves, to others and to the community at large. So, if I have a drug-using mom and, before she's ready to change her use, if she's willing to find another mom to trade-off child care – "you go out and party tonight and I'll watch your kids, and then tomorrow night I'll go out and party and you watch my kids" – I see that as harm reduction. I can give you an extreme example of harm reduction: I was doing a training in Oakland, California, and one of the participants was a social worker with a female client who was dealing drugs. This client had an apartment complex and everyone living there was a mom with children. This client had been collecting all the welfare money of these mom/tenants at the beginning of every month and then doled out drugs to them during the month. She distributed a certain amount of various drugs per day to each of the women. She knew all the tenants' kids' birthdays and they all got acknowledged; she kept the moms off the street and off prostitution, and this approach kept the moms available to care for their children because they didn't have to go hunt down drugs or wind up in jail. Also the moms couldn't be greedy about their drug use; they couldn't get their checks and use up $200 worth of drugs in two days. But they always had enough dope to last through the month, and they all had their kids. This client was making sure - when she collected the money from the moms - that every household had food first and that the kids had everything they needed; she made sure the kids were safe and secure. Now *that's* harm reduction! Of course, this client is a criminal and she's going to get locked up someday, but her concept is an awesome example of harm reduction.

I also want to say that I understand why people have a problem with harm reduction around children, why folks want to insist on abstinence. I do appreciate that children can get harmed in the process of moving toward abstinence or less harmful use, but they also often get harmed when they go into foster care. I can't say which is worse; I think that depends on each individual case. But I really think this woman was looking out for the kids more than we as a society sometimes do when we simply say to users "you have to stop now and do that forever or we'll take your kids." It's just not that simple. And I want to be clear that this particular example isn't helping the addiction cycle of these women. However, is it better then having them turn tricks? YES. Did it reduce the harm to everyone in their family and were there more moms at home than out on the street? YES. And this would be only a beginning - not the end - of helping these women.

Back when I was preparing those addiction classes, the Department of Health and Human Services in Sacramento County's AODTI [Editor's Note: Alcohol and other Drugs Training Institute] training director hired Dr. John McCarthy, who runs Bi-Valley Methadone Clinic in Sacramento, to write part of the curriculum on harm reduction. I remember reading his contribution and thinking that it was kind of dumb because Dr. McCarthy said things like, "include addicts in decision-making processes." I remember thinking, "Oh, that's going to be a really interesting conversation - ha, ha!" Obviously, I still didn't understand harm reduction, but I was getting closer because of my tobacco use.

In AA, abstinence is talked about as the only way, which was definitely the right path for me. How do I know that? I've been a smoker for a long time; I've quit hundreds of times. I've had to because every time I start to think that I can handle smoking again, I go out and start smoking again! Since this was my pattern for years, and since I pay attention to my patterns today, I'm not willing to take a chance with experimenting with trying to safely use other drugs, including alcohol. For me, abstinence is the answer, but it isn't the answer for everyone. My experience with cigarette smoking has helped me understand and appreciate harm reduction more.

I'd say the final piece in my harm reduction education came when I got trained in Motivational Interviewing in 2004 in Portland, Maine. I had been teaching Sacramento County's AODTI classes since 1994, saw the "War on Drugs" film in 1995, was exposed to methadone through Dr. McCarthy around 1995 - all inching me closer to a better understanding of harm reduction. I see methadone as a viable means of treatment, and as harm reducing. I talk about the efficacy of methadone in all of my classes.

I really love AA and truly believe that it saved my life. I haven't attended meetings regularly for 15 years or more, but I still feel like I owe a huge debt to AA. When I talk about methadone to 12-Steppers, I talk about it in a strength context and I say all groups - all people - have strengths and issues. AA is an incredible organization, and it has its issues, as well. It can be very hypercritical about things such as methadone because it says you must be drug free in order to be in recovery, and then it goes further to define what a drug isn't: caffeine and nicotine and sugar are not drugs. You can consume massive quantities of those drugs - five cups of coffee, three packs of cigarettes a day and six pounds of sugar a day - and you're drug free, but if you consume methadone, you're not. The vast majority of AA members will be smoking a cigarette saying, "Be drug free, drug free, drug free."

In the United States, I believe that we have a very solid unspoken policy and it goes something like this: good people do good drugs and bad people do bad drugs. There is a very clear line here between a good drug and a bad drug. There is only one legal dealer and that is the pharmacy, and if you get your drugs from somewhere other than at a pharmacy - or a liquor store - you are bad. AA sometimes does the same thing. AA may pressure someone to get off psychiatric medications or antidepressants or methadone because you're not considered really drug free if you are on medications. According to World Services of AA, medications are acceptable as long as you follow a doctor's orders. Someone handed me a pamphlet from Narcotics Anonymous (NA) a couple of months ago. I couldn't find the date on it, and it literally said that people on methadone should be allowed to attend meetings but should not be allowed to share. I was so pissed that it was in writing, in NA literature! I hope that it is an older pamphlet and not something newer.

In any case, I believe in AA's often-stated philosophy: take what you want and leave the rest. That is exactly what I do. And that's why I absolutely refer people to 12-Step. I tell them that it may not be the perfect thing for them, but if they can get into it, it's phenomenal what you can get out of it. There are other great things about it, too: it's accessible 24 hours a day, it's free, and it's everywhere. Often, too, people in meetings will informally help a newcomer with housing and even employment. My stepdaughter just got arrested last night, and I'm happy. She got arrested and her son was removed. She's going into sober living today, pre-treatment. If she decides to go into 12-Step meetings, I believe it will make her recovery process so much easier. She will have an opportunity to meet healthier people who are trying to make significant changes in their lives. In her current life, every single person she knows - including her family members - use some type of substances. How do you make that cultural shift between the world of drugs and alcohol to the world of people who don't use all alone? 12-Step is an incredibly awesome bridge. So is church, but I couldn't stomach church; I could barely stomach the spiritual part of AA. When I first came into AA I said, "I don't want anything to do with that God crap," and the first thing someone said to me was, "Don't worry about that God stuff; you don't have to. Just don't drink today." How Motivational Interviewing is that? How consistent is that with "you can take what you want and leave the rest?" That worked for me. I understand that some people don't like AA. If you can fit yourself in, and if you don't take everything everyone says as the absolute truth, it can be an incredible place. AA is very early recovery. I do stick my head in a meeting every once in a while just to acknowledge and say I have been clean for 27 years (I was 25 when I got clean) thanks to AA.

I think people in 12-Step recovery have built a lot of the current drug and alcohol treatment, and that's great. And I think the best combination is exactly what you (hopefully) figure out early on in working in the field, which is: *personal experience is a wonderful thing, but without education, can I really be helpful?* And I say when you get both experience and education together, you have a better chance of running a treatment program that's healthy. People straight out of treatment or AA recovery can be as harmful as I was because I was adamant that AA was the only way. And yes, it was for me, but I'm really clear that there are many other paths that are just as good; sadly, not always as available, but just as good. I even believe that some people can learn to drink and use responsibly after having had problems with their drug use because I know enough people in recovery now who are no longer "clean and sober" but who are not alcoholics or addicts either. I have a friend who drinks about 20 beers a year, one at a time. She goes on these incredible hikes with a bunch of other friends and, at the end of the hike, everyone has a beer. She manages fine. I believe people can recover in many ways: on their own, in their own way or, like I did, with AA. It doesn't matter; what matters is that somehow, someway, people find something that helps them reduce the harm in their lives. And that's all that matters.

Pam Smithstan is an educator, consultant, and Motivational Interviewing trainer in the North Bay Area. She can be reached at FSCconsultants@AOL.COM.

DEE-DEE STOUT

12-STEPPING HARM REDUCTIONIST

My journey to harm reduction, like that of many other 12-Stepping harm reductionists, was anything but straight (pun intended). If you had told me even five years ago at the start of this project that I would be calling myself a *harm reductionist*, I would've told you that you were nuts! After all, I wasn't taught much about harm reduction; what I thought I knew was that "harm reduction" meant two things: 1) methadone maintenance and 2) just letting people use. My thinking radically changed after attending my first harm reduction conference in Seattle, Washington, in 2002 to conduct a workshop on Motivational Interviewing. You know, oddly, I found that I felt right at home at that conference, much as I had many years ago in Alcoholics Anonymous (AA). And with that initial personal observation, I began to see that I could indeed be both in AA and a harm reductionist!

Today, students often tell me that what leads to their best understanding harm reduction principles is the statement "all lives are worth saving." It is a phrase at the core of harm reduction principles and one on which all in the field of health and addictions seem to agree. I first heard that phrase from Dan Bigg, director of the Chicago Recovery Alliance (CRA). Dan became one of my guides on the road to harm reduction. Through his invitation to learn more about it, whether through his own presentations or those of others, my mind continued to open, a process that had various "moments of clarity" such as the ones I had when I was getting help from Alan Marlatt while studying relapse prevention during my graduate studies. I once asked Dan if I could come to Chicago to speak to needle exchange participants, and he said yes, as long as I understood that these were people, not some freak show. He made sure I understood how to be accessible to consumers of needle exchange, how to treat them with dignity and respect and how to really listen with compassion to them talk about their lives.

But I digress. So how did I come to even seek out information about harm reduction? Well, because I had to. I think you'll understand what I mean as my story unfolds.

As I look back on it, the first glimpse I had professionally that I needed to make a change was when I took a job in the late 1980's as Women's Director for a large residential aftercare program in Northern California. I was responsible for four women's recovery homes, which in total housed about 60-80 women in some cases with their children. Everything seemed to be going well. We were full most of the time and conducting random searches as well as urinalyses on a regular basis to be sure the houses were "safe." The women were required to look for work and to attend both house meetings and 12-Step meetings at minimum several times a week. We also held house family group meetings where we discussed topics such as parenting and sober fun and arranged for picnics and other activities that were designed especially to include the children. One day, after a particularly dramatic evening at one of the houses, I had become completely frustrated by one of the clients and her two children, the latter having started a fire in one of the houses "just for fun." While I don't recall *what* I said to her, I will never forget *how* I said it: I absolutely screamed at her, so much so that I actually scared myself. In that moment, I realized that I needed two things: 1) more recovery and 2) more education. To my credit, I left that job and went back to school within weeks. However, the damage was done to that client and her children (I might add here that my boss was not at all upset at my outburst; in fact, he was pleased as he felt she deserved it as far he was concerned due to the possibility of harm to both his property and the other residents). At this point, I was sober about nine months, and I had just been accepted at San Francisco State University to complete my undergraduate degree. I had no further drug and alcohol education other than what I had learned during my own alcohol and other drug treatment.

One of the many things I questioned during this time was the idea of "character defects." One half of the Drs. Marsh team, who were both my mentors and long-time AA sponsors, Dr. Earle Marsh (author, *Physician, Heal Thyself*[55]) had often told me how much he disliked this term. He used to say, "People are not defective, they are simply emotionally stunted." I appreciated the difference as I felt that if I were defective, there would be no reason to try to change. However, if I were simply stunted in my growth, that was changeable even if it would take time. But this concept of character defects is a large part of the 12-Step philosophy of AA and suggests that one must acknowledge how their own actions may have contributed to the problems with addiction that they are now facing. Sometimes this concept can also be quite damaging. For instance, early in my recovery, after sharing at a meeting, I was told by another member to "look for my part in things" when discussing my sexual assault at age twelve[56]. Today I know that I was a child, without "defects," simply searching for love in all the wrong places, as the old song goes, and not responsible for the harms that came to me (harm reduction strategies have no such "moral inventory").

The next time I recall thinking about harm reduction was after burning out from clinical work several years ago. I had worked "in the trenches" for about eight years and suddenly found that I dreaded going to work and went home exhausted every day. I just couldn't take the daily fights anymore - with insurance companies, patients, families, you name it. At this time, I was working in hospital-based residential treatment, which meant we were seeing some of the most challenging and complicated cases, as insurance had clamped down on addiction treatment benefits by this time (this was in the early-to-mid 1990's). I had completed my master's degree in health counseling by then and had become a California-certified drug and alcohol counselor. I had quite a bit of education and training and, at that point, many years of experience in the field. But I was beginning to question how we were doing treatment as I read more about clinical trials and searched for evidence that the treatments we were using actually worked (at this point, outcomes in treatment were being discussed by providers, likely due to managed care). I didn't really understand all these concepts, but somehow I felt they were important and therefore I kept reading and listening. I began to question things at work and found my ambivalence difficult to cope with, as I knew there was a deep love for patients from myself and other staff, but was that enough?

Finally, I had become so stressed at trying to fit in at work - but then challenging everything - that I knew I had to leave. It was very hard on me to see that the place that I felt had given me life - where I had begun my own recovery - now felt confining and confusing (I was working in the hospital where I had been in treatment years before). The difference between how we said we were treating patients and the reality of what we were actually doing was too great for me to tolerate anymore – including my own behavior. But I had also learned some important lessons there including this saying, one of my favorites: "People don't care how much you know until they first know how much you care."[57] But I had no idea what else to do or even where to go to find alternatives (I still didn't know any existed). All I knew was that the work I loved was killing me. My doctor insisted on stress leave as I plunged into suicidality and depression.

I wound up leaving the counseling field completely and finding a job in marketing for a residential treatment facility in Northern California. During a regular staff meeting there with our marketing director, I was told about this training being offered by Dr. William Miller (co-author, *Motivational Interviewing*[58]) and associates at the University of New Mexico in Albuquerque. The training was a NIDA (National Institute of Drug Abuse) study that involved learning Motivational Interviewing (MI) and was several days long. My boss encouraged me to apply, which I did, not quite sure what to expect or even if this was the best thing for me to do. After all, I had left clinical work except for my private practice, so why even do this? But I had read the book, and I had attended a training in Seattle with Dr. James Prochaska, the co-developer of the now famous Transtheoretical Model of the Stages of Change Theory. And I loved the stages of change! So much so that before I would even accept the marketing position, I asked the director about the clinical use of the stages of change theory and if they had more than just AA to offer patients. So, I guess I was well on my way into this new thinking called harm reduction – well, new to me – though I didn't really know what to do with all of it and certainly didn't call it harm reduction. Yet something in my gut felt right about these concepts of engagement. I was hearing mantras such as "all lives are worth saving" and "a little change is better than none" and that "there are other ways to recover besides AA." Hmmm...the wheels, they were a' turning; there'd be no going back now!

One of the requirements for application to this Motivational Interviewing training was the submission of an audiotaped session with a new client. I didn't have much time to accomplish this as the deadline was quickly approaching. The client I had in mind for this was having big problems with his heroin use and, while he had some desire to quit, he had little desire for treatment. The night of our appointment happened to coincide with the last opportunity for a session in order to mail the tape out in time for the application's deadline. And, as Murphy's Law would have it, the client called, very high on heroin and apologetically saying, "You really don't want me to come in; I'm all f***ed up." Now I admit that part of my thinking was about my own need for this tape, but I also knew this young man and his family, and I knew that he stood to lose everything I knew was important to him if he didn't find a way to put the heroin down. So, I took a deep breath and said, "Yes, I do. Come on in anyway!" The minute I put that phone down I thought, "Oh good grief, what have I done??" I had just crossed a sacred line in alcohol and other drugs counseling. Ethically, the only thing worse than seeing a client when they were using drugs was to have sexual relations with them. This is not accurate, of course, but that's how enormous my decision was to me and my colleagues - and there was no turning back. That was the first time I had knowingly worked with someone under the influence of drugs, although who knows how many times it happened *without* my knowledge! Well, I got into the MI training and the rest is history.

Oh, do you want to know what happened to that client? Well, he saw me a couple more times and then, within two weeks of that taped session (and before I knew I was going to the MI training), he called me - to ask me if I would honor him by driving him to residential treatment! It took my breath away. When I asked him what had changed, he said that he so appreciated my willingness to see him even when "at his worst" that he felt compelled to truthfully look at his life - at how much he actually had to lose – and make a change; that I was the only drug counselor he ever saw who was willing to see him while under the influence of drugs and that made his life feel worthy of reconsideration. Incredible! By the way, the last time I saw this client, he was still in traditional abstinence recovery, married with more children and had recently finished seminary.

Now you can say, "well, that's only one story and there are always exceptions!" That's what I thought, too. But I now know that's exactly the point! As clinicians, we need to be uncovering those *exceptions* - the exceptions to the problems our clients are experiencing instead of always focusing on the problem, or rushing to fix it. I've always been told – and I believed - that working with people when they are loaded is futile, worthless and perhaps even harmful. But this incident really got my attention and amplified my curiosity about this thing called "harm reduction." It also led to the removal from my office policy a statement that required sobriety to come to session. Then I went to Chicago to collectively study with Jane Peller, John Walters, and Scott Miller [Editor's note: Peller & Walters are the authors of *Recreating Brief Therapy* (2000; WW Norton) and Scott Miller is the author of several books, including *The Heroic Client* (2000; Jossey-Bass) and *The Heart and Soul of Change: What Works in Therapy* (2005; APA). Scott can be reached through www.talkingcure.com]- another group of brilliant people who would make my head hurt even more as my known world, both personally and professionally, was challenged more than I thought possible.

The final piece of undoing to my traditional thinking occurred during a lunch with Jeannie Little, now the Executive Director of the Harm Reduction Therapy Center in San Francisco (and co-author of *Over the Influence*[59]). At that time, Jeannie and I were acquainted due to our work on a grant project with the Department of Public Health, then Community Substance Abuse Services (now Community Behavioral Health Services). I was still in my marketing position, so I asked her to lunch both to discuss harm reduction and to ask about the marketing potential for my new skills in Motivational Interviewing (I didn't really see the full connection of MI to harm reduction at the time). I recall asking Jeannie to tell me more about this thing called harm reduction - you know, what was it really? I also told her that I was really tired of fighting with clients and that having only one way to recover (abstinence and 12-Step) just didn't make sense to me anymore. I remember she laughed and said, "Well another one bites the dust!" Presumably concerned that she had just insulted me, she went on to explain that her outburst was due to excitement and sheer joy and not meant as an insult, due to hearing my "questions about the status quo in treatment" - and the possibility of another mind being expanded, I suspect!

Well, I continued to study with Jeannie and her partner, Patt Denning (author, *Harm Reduction Psychotherapy*[60]; co-author, *Over the Influence*). I took classes at the Harm Reduction Coalition and read everything I could. I also began to find and speak to others in my field of alcohol and other drugs treatment who practiced harm reduction. What I learned was that harm reduction could be quite complicated. And it is anything but "anything goes." Harm reduction is an organized series of strategies designed to reduce the harmful effects of alcohol and other drugs and behaviors to individuals, their families, and society at large. I also began to see some bits of harm reduction in AA, as well. For example, AA never says you *must* stop your drinking or even that you should; it simply suggests that theirs is "A" way to live and then invites you to "come on back" if "you want what we have found." It never suggests that it has all the answers for everyone or even for all alcohol problems. In fact, the book *Alcoholics Anonymous* discusses how you come to AA "when all else fails...." AA also says, "take what works and leave the rest." In reading more about the history of AA's founders, I found men who wanted to create a safe haven, a place to come for those people for whom nothing else seemed to work and society deemed hopeless: those at their absolute "bottom." But even for them, AA doesn't claim a cure. In fact, the only thing AA has ever guaranteed is a spiritual awakening[61]. Period.

The last chink in my old Minnesota Medical Model armor was thrown off when about ten years ago I was diagnosed with a condition called *fibromyalgia syndrome* (FMS). It is a chronic, potentially debilitating, extremely painful condition of the fascia (the soft connective tissue) and muscles of the body that appears to be connected to neurochemical anomalies in the brain, possibly genetic kidney malfunctioning and, most certainly, historical trauma. After a very long process of trial-and-error treatments with numerous wonderful (and not so wonderful) health professionals, I took the advice of my primary care physician and began taking long-acting medications for pain relief, as I had to return to work (I had been on disability the better part of three years and ran out of benefits). The discussions with my doctor and other health care professionals, as well as numerous friends, leading up this decision were some of the most difficult of my life, causing me unbelievable stress and emotional pain. After so many years of traditional (read *complete abstinence*) recovery, I struggled with the voices in my head telling me, on the one hand, I was "using" and, on the other, that I needed to listen to the experts and take this medication to potentially *keep* me from using something else; plus, it might actually improve my life.

Sadly, I found that the very people in 12-Step that I shared this difficult process with were now the same people who in private – and not so private - were vilifying me for "using." They acted as if I had just shot up heroin for giggles and went on some sort of spree. I actually had someone come up to me at an AA meeting once, after I had talked about my struggles with depression and pain, and say, "You know, you just need to make a gratitude list." I was completely insulted and confused. It seemed unbelievable that they didn't really hear just how much pain I was in, or perhaps they just didn't believe me. Either way, I knew these comments weren't in the spirit of AA, but I also knew, sadly, that I couldn't freely discuss my struggles in the very place to which I'd always turned.

Today, I still struggle at times with the use of medications, even ones for the bipolar disorder that I also have. At those times, I do my best to remember something Patt Denning once said to me, regarding a simple way to look at drug use of any kind: "Is your life better with this drug (medication or other) or without?" I love that question! I know that today – *for me* - the answer is that my life is *definitely* better with properly taken medications and a medical team that helps me to supervise myself. In fact, there would be no life, as I would describe life, were it not for the medications -- because I tried. And yet, from time to time I still have to say to myself, "you have a legitimate, legally-defined disability that causes unbearable pain constantly if you don't take your medication properly. I do not misuse medications and, for now, this is the best life I can make for myself. I am in recovery!" I am also never euphoric nor completely without pain - ever.

I know there are some people who truly believe I would be better off on SSI and – their words - completely "clean & sober" (read *drug-free*) rather than on *any* medication. And I'd like to ask them, "just whose life would be better if I did that? Do you believe the pain will magically disappear? Or the bipolar disorder? Isn't that magical thinking, too?" I will never forget an old friend of mine in AA may years ago, Mike (to whom I dedicated this book), who struggled constantly over many years trying to achieve continuous, permanent sobriety. Mike would put together a few days or weeks here and there and then, inevitably, come back to the meeting, raising his hand again as a newcomer (those who have a relapse or are new to AA are asked to identify themselves as a newcomer, ostensibly to welcome them, not to shame them). Finally, Mike had gone to see a psychiatrist who placed him on various medications. After some time on these medications, Mike began to look better and had even managed to remain continuously sober for several months. He was working again, smiling in meetings and seemed happy for the first time in the nearly four years I had known him. But at some point, he again began to struggle with the idea that he shouldn't be taking medications, that to do so meant he wasn't really "clean," as some AA members were apparently telling him. One day a man, who had been sober a long time and coming regularly to this particular AA meeting, told him to "get off that crap if you *really* want to be sober!" Mike did. And in short order, also committed suicide. When his roommate came to the meeting to tell us of our collective loss, this same man said aloud, "Well, at least he died sober." I will never forget that and how sickened I was – I am - by those words.

I have also lost some friends and colleagues in my life due to my use of medications; I am sad for that. But I don't understand how these folks believed that abandoning me when I needed them most was somehow helpful to me, somehow the right thing to do – or the *AA* thing to do. That's not the AA I love. So today, I have had to hide my medical status from many in the field. I can't work in most treatment facilities due to the medications I have to take as I would fail the drug test even though I am considered to be an incredible educator and a highly regarded, skilled clinician in my field. And what really confuses me is how is this narrow, rigid thinking *recovery?* What kind of recovery is that?

Coming to harm reduction was a *kicking and screaming* effort for me even though I see that I was already on the road. Gratefully, I was taught that "doing recovery gracefully isn't important, but doing it is." I have certainly not been graceful in my recovery - but I understand the point of the saying: it is not important *how* you recover, only that you do – *recover* your own life, in whatever way and by whatever means works for you. I've come to learn that "recovery" means three simple things: *connectedness, mindfulness, and inner growth.* In other words, be connected to yourself and others; pay attention as best you can and as often as you can;

and do whatever you can to keep growing in life. By this definition *anyone*, including those still using substances, can be in recovery as long as their life is improving and by their measure. I like to call this "*harm reduction recovery*" which I verbally distinguish from "*traditional recovery"* (meaning abstinence), and I hope for the day when this can all just be called *recovery - whatever* that means to the individual. In the meantime, I simply know that I am recovering from my previous life, and from my present one. And, even if my vocabulary about it has improved I seem to be back where I began this crazy recovering life-journey: appreciating people for their struggles, seeing the differences between preferences and problems, finding compassion in the world and in me, and being optimistic about life: being connected, mindful, and growing. So let me end here with another AA saying that I think fits: "Be careful what you pray for; you might just get it!" I think I have.

Dee-Dee Stout (author) is currently on faculty at City College of San Francisco; Clinical Program Manager at Project Pride in Oakland, CA; and Director of Responsible Recovery, a strength-based, client-centered consulting, coaching, and training group, focused on Motivational Interviewing and trauma. She can be reached through her website at www.responsiblerecovery.org.

TOMMIE (LARRY) WALTON

12-STEPPING HARM REDUCTIONIST

Let me start with a little history about my first recollections about alcohol. The first experience I recall involving alcohol was with my paternal step-grandfather who lived in a small community in South Georgia. He was the town blacksmith, and I spent a lot of time with this man, working with him and selling watermelons by the side of the road in town. I remember every morning he would start off with what he called a "hot toddy." I watched him for a long time and then, when I got old enough (maybe four or five), he would stand me up and invite me to take a sip before he downed it. Although I don't remember whether I liked the taste or not, it was certainly an enjoyable experience. The next alcohol-related experience I recall was while I was living with my parents. My dad was working on a PhD, and, while eating dinner and drinking, he almost died due to choking on a piece of his dinner. He was intoxicated and hadn't chewed his food well enough before swallowing it. So I had these opposing experiences: one very positive memory and one very frightening memory, both with very important people in my life.

The next alcohol-related experience I recall was at the age of 13 or 14. It was summertime in Georgia - very hot - and we were in a new house my parents had recently built. We were sprigging the front yard with southern turf grass, and my father was having some beers on this Saturday while we worked. Someone unexpectedly came to visit and my father immediately stopped what he was doing, hiding the beer he was drinking under his car in the carport. I thought, "What was that all about?" Those are things about alcohol that remain in my vivid and easily recalled memory.

At about the age of 15, I decided that I should probably start drinking as a lot of my peers were doing it. It was a Carling's Black Label in the back seat of a 1955 Chevrolet that was owned by a friend of mine - I think I had left home about midnight that night; I was being initiated into a relationship with alcohol. Alcohol was a perfect fit for me immediately somehow and, by the time I was 16, I was experiencing enough symptoms that, in hindsight, I now know I had become a high-risk user, if not alcohol dependent already. I was drinking to the point of acute intoxication every time I drank. I continued that pattern, escalating to about the age of 21 when I moved to Tucson, Arizona. That was in about 1967 when I was enrolled in the University of Arizona at Tucson to study geology.

Interestingly enough, at about that time, the flower child hippie movement was greeting me in Tucson. I had married and moved almost immediately to Tucson. It became apparent to me that my new spouse, who didn't really know me that well, was not going to tolerate my drinking. So, I moved into a period of controlled drinking where I substituted alcohol with other drugs that were becoming widespread and easily accessible. It was 1967, after all! I took advantage of this accessibility and used other drugs as a replacement for alcohol from about 1967 until around 1979. The marker for my sense of control was that I could have one drink on any occasion - as long as I didn't drink it! I would walk around with this one drink all night at a party, confident ironically in my knowledge of being completely out of control with alcohol. I would walk around others who were drunk or stoned or so geeked up on something that they didn't know if it was my first or my 15th drink. But I knew, and I knew I wasn't going to drink it. It was crazy, but it worked for me. When I think about that time in terms of harm reduction, that was a harm reduction methodology for me.

It became apparent to me one particular night about 12 years later that I'd done enough experimenting of this controlled drinking and using. Much like my father's experience as a functional alcoholic, I, too, was functioning: I had finished college, I had gotten a graduate degree, I was married, I had a couple of kids and I was employed in my chosen occupation. But one night, I was at a party with maybe 20 or 30 other professional people and I had my usual one drink. I looked around and realized nobody was really having a conversation with anybody. Everybody was just waiting. Something really hit me that said, "You know, you have really done enough of this." I had also been running a mental health and substance abuse treatment center, surrounded by a lot of recovering people. I had noticed that people seemed to be getting along in life more smoothly than I was, and I began to wonder if that could have anything to do with all these drugs I was using to substitute and control my alcohol intake the way I did. So, I decided that I ought to try complete abstinence this time. The next day became my sobriety date. I went immediately to AA.

So, into AA I went. It really freaked me out, too. AA was in its infancy in 1979 in the community in which I was working at the time: Athens, Georgia. There might have been one meeting that met twice a week, not like the thousands each week today, but there was a new AA clubhouse that had been formed. There, I again saw the man responsible for the acceleration of 12-Step in Athens (I had met him earlier, probably in about 1974) and he offered to come to my agency to do some outreach. Little did I know then that the real outreach would be for me! He told me his story, and it made an impression on me in terms of his character and his story - the way he lived his life. He kept very subtly mentoring me for about the next six years until I "got it." I think he was meeting me where I was at, giving me information that I was seeking in a way, but he was careful to never direct it specifically at me. He would simply tell me his story and tell me about his experiences with other people. He was really sharing his experience, strength and hope with me as we say in AA, both verbally and behaviorally because, when he showed up, he was also demonstrating what recovery could be. This was completely in the tradition of "attraction rather than promotion" that AA endorses. Eventually, I got a sponsor and went to lots of meetings my sponsor held, including couples meetings at his home that were really unofficial Couples AA. My wife at the time and I regularly attended a home group. That was 1979. And I probably continued that up until 1995. I was pretty active. I didn't go to meetings every day, but I went frequently - more days than not. My kids were older at that time, and so I began to wean myself away from 12-Step in part to get more involved in other areas of my life.

The programs that we were offering at my agency were fairly traditional, abstinence-based programs, and what I knew phenomenologically from working in the treatment field for some time was that most people didn't get 12-Step right away; they didn't get *recovery* right away. Also, some of them used 12-Step to get better and some of them didn't; some got better with 12-Step and some got better without it. We had a philosophy at the agency that we would take anybody, anytime - we understood that, as we weren't gods, we didn't know when some miracle might happen, but we sure didn't want to be responsible for nixing the opportunity when that miracle lightning might strike! We had folks who must have gone through detox fifty or sixty times. Some who had detoxed that many times later died in trailer fires, burning themselves up by falling asleep while intoxicated. We had people that we detoxed that many times that found recovery – they "got it" - and are sober today. We had people that did it with AA, some that didn't, and some that still haven't tried. And the AA community back then was very open to all of these folks and to alternative ideas, appreciative of the many roads folks may take to get to recovery. The AA community has changed much since that first meeting I attended in 1979.

Today's AA has become a lot less tolerant. NA (Narcotics Anonymous) had started up in the community, and there seemed to be some kind of competition between AA and NA leading to a lot of division. There was a division between "old timers" and "newcomers." There was a division between those who got their recovery on the street and with 12-Step only and those who started their recovery in treatment facilities. AA became more rigid and, as it became rigid, I noticed that certain groups of people felt uncomfortable there. I felt there was almost the sense that the requirement for participation had become a mandate that one *must* stop drinking, rather than a suggestion that one have a desire to stop drinking. In fact, in some meetings if you mentioned you were anything but an alcoholic - such as saying, "Hi, my name is Larry and I'm an alcoholic and addict" - you might be asked to leave that meeting, possibly even admonished severely for even attending. When this began to happen, it caused me to decrease my frequency at meetings because I realized how lucky I had been: AA really "took me where I was" in those days. I worked the program of the 12-Steps at my own pace, not someone else's. No one tried to fix me in any direct way in those days, and I was offered many choices about whether I attended meetings or not and how often I came. When I attended meetings, the discussions were very non-directive, merely *suggestive* as it states in the early writings about AA and how it works. People just came from their "experience, strength and hope," and I could take it or leave it. Folks at these early meetings really seemed to believe that if I didn't "get it" today that was OK - I could get it tomorrow or next week or next year or ten years from now. It was up to me. That old AA phrase of "take what you need and leave the rest" was very helpful to me then. And I see harm reduction much like that.

Harm reduction works by attraction and not promotion, just like AA. Something is offered or suggested and people take it when they're ready or never take it at all. It's all up to the individual, with some guidance if they allow. There is a sense of personal responsibility and accountability for one's recovery and the way in which you get recovery. This means also that there are lots of different ways to recover and many different supports available for people who are interested in seeking ways to recover. Recovery then becomes simply "getting better." It is a process, not a complete destination. And it is found in many places, not just in the rooms of 12-Step meetings or treatment centers. I believe - no, I *know* -- that one can come out the other side with a higher quality of life as a result of one's experiences using alcohol and other drugs by making a decision to learn from those experiences, not simply discounting it all as "worthless time spent as a junkie or drunk." It can even help to inform other decisions in your life by facilitating how you see your life in general: negatively or positively. And this is very harm reductionistic, seeing the strengths in the individual before you see the challenges. So the outcome – the "other side" - is really variable, different for each individual. AA, like harm reduction, in my experience, tells people to take as much or as little of what it has to offer that's helpful to the person or take nothing at all. As we say "take what you need and leave the rest!" Both concepts also support the idea that some people might require outside help and they are encouraged to seek it in both harm reduction and in the original writings of AA. That's another thing that's distressful about AA today: there is a real tendency for it to be a closed system nowadays regarding outside help - like medications or therapy – rather than the open system that I knew and love.

I have come to look at 12-Step and various recoveries as a patchwork quilt. You know, lots of different people may stitch in a single piece of the quilt and any single individual patch probably isn't the final piece of the quilt of the person's life and recovery. As a professional or a person working 12-Step, I do a good job stitching in patches of quilts for others, as was done for me. That's really all I can do. That and continue to work on my own and still occasionally ask for others to work on a piece with me. I might only get the opportunity to stitch in one piece of someone's quilt, and I may never get to see any quilts completed. And that's okay; I don't have to complete their quilt or hurry it along so I can feel like I've done my job. It really goes to that notion of being not-God. We do the stitching; the miracles are really up to God, not me, whatever that miracle is. And I like that because it means I don't have to worry about the outcome because my job is just to do the stitching.

Tommie (Larry) Walton is the Director of Recovery Café in Athens, Georgia. He can be reached at recoverycafe@gmail.com. For more on Recovery Café, go to www.recoverycafe.com.

IMANI WOODS

12-STEPPING HARM REDUCTIONIST

My initial work in this field was with the homeless of New York. I was a social worker in the department of Health and Human Services for about three and a half years. I then left my job to go to work for the Health and Hospitals Corporation. This was my practicum for substance abuse counseling. I stayed with them for about a year and a half at which time I returned to the HRA [Editor's note: the Human Resources Administration], working in homeless shelters until I left for good to move to Seattle. I never did work as a treatment counselor except during my practicum. That was enough for me! I guess you could say I didn't believe that being a counselor was my destiny. But I am grateful for the experience because I believe it added to my credibility.

In 1981, I became sober. I was a very, very sick and confused drug addict. I went to AA, but I never really took it very seriously; I just "drank the Kool-Aid" so to speak. You know, I gave a talk one time, preaching that AA was the solution and believed what I was saying. I now think I know why it works and what it is – and what it isn't. For instance, AA is not a detoxification center. I try to tell people what AA is for, that it has one purpose: to help individuals who wish to sustain a drug and alcohol free lifestyle. Period.

You know, I really have a hard time in this line of work with people constantly telling *everyone* their background – self-disclosure. I don't like it at all. It seems to me that this constant disclosure has only succeeded in separating us and creating a disturbing, fuzzy area where we say because you used to get high, you know more than so and so. Basically, I think that just because you've gotten high, you don't necessarily have better insight as a counselor as someone who hasn't! My sponsor used to tell me that the only 12-Step work is work you don't get paid for, so volunteer, but that wasn't for me. Again, I think that helps set up a dichotomy that isn't good for us, you know when this one knows better because she got high and that one's no better because she didn't.

When I started not punishing people because they got high, I then started moving towards approaches other than abstinence only. For instance, let's look at the concept of denial as we usually think of it. I was working in a women's shelter with people who had decided to use drugs. For them, it was clearly a primary preference in life. They *knew* what they were doing. I really disagree with people who think that addicts don't know what they're doing. Addicts aren't ignorant; they know what they're doing. Denial to me is the kind of a thing that exists in a person of means, someone who has other resources around them. The average addict/alcoholic isn't in *denial*. Denial runs a poor second to *rationalization*. Denial tells me "no, it's not there." Rationalization tells me "well, I know they're going to find out, but if so and so wouldn't have done such and such, then I would be okay." If we didn't rationalize, then we would have to actually *do* something! Now there are exceptions to this, like everything else: for instance, people who have been traumatized. In those cases, there is a certain amount of rationalization. Being able to rationalize in those situations is what's keeping these folks alive and then it may move into self- medication. And, by the way, I don't see rationalization as a negative term. Again, rationalization for some is what keeps some people alive!

So when did I *really* enter harm reduction? I was working at King's County Hospital, Seattle and, therefore, I was able to attend a training put on by the State and NIDA [Editor's Note: the National Institute of Drug Abuse]. Edith Springer was the instructor. Edie was teaching courses on HIV and substance abuse, and suddenly I could see treatment in another way. That day I was able to keep my mind open enough to listen.

You know, I knew that treatment worked. And I'm definitely not one of those people that will get in the middle of the fight regarding which treatment is better than the other. I also know that harm reduction is excellent. And, on the public heath continuum, harm reduction should be at the *beginning* of a health intervention. I believe harm reduction *is* public health, in the truest sense of that phrase. I also think that harm reduction and abstinence are compatible in the United States. Abstinence can be a part of harm reduction, so harm reduction is NOT incompatible with abstinence. We need to remember that harm reduction doesn't mean you just let people use on the premises and not kick them out, although that's what some treatment facilities that have implemented harm reduction think. That's actually increasing harm! It all just tells me that a lot of people don't really understand harm reduction at all. And that's dangerous.

When I went back to HRA, having left Health and Hospital, things started to change for me. I began to do a lot more work with people who had HIV. And I started to realize that not everybody was getting sober! Through this new work, I began to realize that we should be able to do something for everyone. I just never agreed with the notion that people should just go in and out of treatment "until they get it." I felt that I found a way to justify the little bit of work I did. I no longer thought, "Whoever doesn't get any abstinence doesn't deserve any care."

Basically that's how I started working towards harm reduction. And I do mean "towards." I believe harm reduction isn't something most of us "get" all at once. Much like recovery, it is a process not a destination. And I *still* believe that AA is incredible, the way it works. AA has its place - it just doesn't work for that many people. But let's also remember that AA is not treatment, although some people wrongly call it that. I mean, I remember being in a group once where they spoke about NA [Editor's Note: Narcotics Anonymous] meetings where you can't talk about anything but drugs; that's really senseless. How could that possibly be treatment?! But having it free is good. Just look at the amount of money being made in these treatment centers. It's no wonder they don't want to change, huh?

Imani Woods is an urban practitioner, Lead Trainer, and Principle of Progressive Solutions in Seattle, Washington. She can be reached through their website at www.harmreductioninblack.org.

IN CONCLUSION

So, where are we here in the US regarding harm reduction these days? I'd say confused! As the federal government continues to refuse to support work on harm reduction (you cannot use the term *harm reduction* in a government grant application or a government-sponsored conference and get financing), it funds more clinical trials on Motivational Interviewing than any other single health intervention. This is certainly ironic since MI can surely be described as harm reduction, as it offers options and encourages a non-judgmental approach to helping people make healthy changes in their lives. I hope that in the course of reading this book, you've gotten a glimpse of an answer to the complicated question of how all the animosity towards harm reduction arose. And that you've been able to see just how much harm reduction there is in the treatment field, especially in the 12-Step world.

I'm also going to ask, after this journey that we've taken together through harm reduction and abstinence-based treatment, that you join with me in looking at the difference between harm reduction and abstinence-only treatment in another way. I suggest that the opposite of abstinence-focused treatment is not harm reduction but, ironically, the adoption of the *zero tolerance approach*. I make this suggestion because zero tolerance demands absolute perfection – no drug (including alcohol) use ever again - and when one fails to meet that singular prescribed goal of perfection, no further treatment is offered (if one has even been able to gain access to an initial treatment episode[62]).

So people grappling with addiction who fail to maintain total sobriety are ostracized and isolated, exiled from the support they so critically need and deserve. Surely, this is 180 degrees removed from the basic, humane tenets of AA as was discussed in these pages. Practitioners in the "abstinence camp" know that relapses or setbacks are the rule and not the exception when making any behavior changes and that these setbacks occur for nearly all clients, especially those attempting abstinence. So this makes achieving abstinence the *exception* to treatment not the norm! In other words, those who manage to be abstinent, especially after one treatment episode, are complete miracles!

The zero tolerance approach is also, of course, completely opposite to the principles of harm reduction that define addiction, or chaotic drug use, as part of a continuum that begins with no use (abstinence) or responsible use, moves to moderate use, then proceeds to problematic use and ends up at chaotic use or dependence and can then, with treatment, move back the other way toward solutions that can include abstinence, responsible use or other options. For those working in the harm reduction paradigm, nothing is prescribed and all options are individualized, including the possibility of abstinence. Furthermore, addicts seeking help are never abandoned when they "fall off the wagon."

It would seem, then, that with relapse the norm and perfect abstinence the exception, the punitive sanctions that zero tolerance demands against the norm are not only the opposite of any form of treatment (including a 12-Step-based program), but ridiculous at best, and unethical at worst. Why would we, to return to our discussion of William White's comment in my Introduction to this book, "create a closed club whose exclusiveness would leave many suffering people refused entry at its doorway?" Since we know from government research that, in general, the longer one stays in treatment the better the outcome, surely the goal is to keep those seeking treatment *in* treatment and not refuse them help just when they need it the most, i.e., when they inevitably slip up?

So where does this book and the voices within it leave us? Well, I hope with a better understanding of harm reduction and 12-Step - especially of AA and its harm reduction origins - and of how some people have made the cultural shift to a more inclusive treatment world (the 12-Stepping Harm Reductionists) or just found themselves in that "other" world in the first place (the Oldtimers). Whatever you may have gained from this little book, I hope you have taken away something of value for your personal life and your professional life. Perhaps it's a clearer understanding of those parts of our field you always wondered about or maybe it's a new way of thinking about treatment, about AA or about harm reduction. It's a new world today and, in that new world, I'd like to think that we have room for more than one way of treating addictions and other related health behaviors. I have never advocated that we get rid of 12-Step. In fact, I am most grateful to it! We simply know that no singular treatment is ever the right treatment for everyone. So perhaps we can take a page from Motivational Interviewing and avoid more argumentation by rolling with whatever resistance might remain after reading this. Or perhaps we should look to AA and its Responsibility Prayer: "When anyone, anywhere reaches out for help, I want the hand of AA always to be there. And for that, I am responsible." I'd like to offer another version of this: "When anyone, anywhere reaches out for help with *any* behavior change, I want there to be many different hands to always be there. And for that, I will be responsible."   Will you join me?

A FEW RESOURCES

Websites for Interviewees

- www.habitdoc.com (Marc Kern)
- Harm Reduction Coalition: www.harmreduction.org (Allan Clear)
- Harm Reduction Therapy Center: www.harmreductiontherapy.org (Jeannie Little and Patt Denning)
- Harm Reduction Psychotherapy and Training Associates: www.andrewtatarsky.com (Andrew Tatarsky)
- Motivational Interviewing: www.motivationalinterview.org and www.williamrmiller.net (Bill Miller)
- www.peele.net (Stanton Peele)
- www.anypositivechange.org (Dan Bigg & Chicago Recovery Alliance-CRA)
- http://depts.washington.edu/abrc/index.htm Addictive Behaviors Research Center (G. Alan Marlatt)
- www.edreedsings.com (Edward Reed)
- www.drugpolicy.org (Chuck Ries)
- Responsible Recovery: www.responsiblerecovery.org (Dee-Dee Stout)

Additional Information

- Alcoholics Anonymous: www.alcoholics-anonymous.org
- Melanie Solomon: www.aanottheonlyway.com

Interviewed Authors: Partial Book List

A. Thomas Horvath

Horvath, A.T. (1998). *Sex, Drugs, Gambling, & Chocolate: A Workbook for Overcoming Addictions.* Impact Publishers, Atascadero, CA.

Ogilvie, H., Horvath, A.T., Rotgers, F. (2002). *Alternatives To Alcoholism: A New Look at Alcoholism and the Choices in Treatment.* Hatherleigh Press, New Ed Edition.

G. Alan Marlatt

Marlatt, G. A., & Gordon, J. R. (1985). *Relapse prevention: maintenance strategies in the treatment of addictive behaviors*. The Guilford clinical psychology and psychotherapy series. New York: Guilford Press.

Marlatt, G. A. (1998). *Harm reduction: pragmatic strategies for managing high risk behaviors*. New York: Guilford Press.

Tucker, J. A., Donovan, D. M., & Marlatt, G. A. (1999). *Changing addictive behavior: bridging clinical and public health strategies*. New York: Guilford Press.

Daley, D. C., & Marlatt, G. A. (2006). *Overcoming your alcohol or drug problem: effective recovery strategies : therapist guide*. Treatments that work. Oxford: Oxford University Press.

Witkiewitz, K., & Marlatt, G. A. (2007). *Therapist's guide to evidence-based relapse prevention*. Practical resources for the mental health professional. Amsterdam: Elsevier Academic Press.

Bill Miller

Miller, W. R. (1995). *Motivational enhancement therapy manual: a clinical research guide for therapists treating individuals with alcohol abuse and dependence*. NIH publication, no. 94-3723. Rockville, Md. (6000 Executive Blvd., Rockville 20892-7003): U.S. Dept. of Health and Human Services, Public Health Service, National Institutes of Health, National Institute on Alcohol Abuse and Alcoholism.

Miller, W. R., & Rollnick, S. (2002). *Motivational interviewing: preparing people for change*. New York: Guilford Press

Miller, W. R., & Munoz, R. F. (2004). *Controlling Your Drinking*. New York: Guilford Press.

Miller, W. R., & Carroll, K. (2006). *Rethinking substance abuse: what the science shows, and what we should do about it*. New York: Guilford Press.

Patt Denning & Jeannie Little (HRTC)

Denning, P. (2000). *Practicing harm reduction psychotherapy: an alternative approach to addictions*. New York: Guilford Press.

Denning, P., Little, J., & Glickman, A. (2004). *Over the influence: the harm reduction guide for managing drugs and alcohol.* New York: Guilford Press.

Marc Kern
Coombs, R. H. (2001). *Addiction recovery tools: a practical handbook.* Thousand Oaks, Calif: Sage Publications.

Rotgers, F., Kern, M.F. & Hoeltzel, R. (2002). *Responsible Drinking: A Moderation Management Approach for Problem Drinkers.* Berkeley: New Harbinger.

Stanton Peele
Peele, S. (1992 Ed.). *The Truth About Addiciton and Recovery.* Fireside Books.

Peele, S. (1999 Ed.) *The Diseasing of America: How We Allowed Recovery Zealots and the Treatment Industry to Convince Us We're Out of Control.* San Francisco: Jossey-Bass.

Peele, S., Bufe, C., Brodsky, A., Horvath, A.T. (2000 Ed.). *Resisting 12-Step Coercion: How to Fight Forced Participation in AA, NA, or 12-Step Treatment.* See Sharp Press.

Peele, S. (2007). *Addiction-Proof Your Child.* Three Rivers Press.

Fred Rotgers
Rotgers, F., Kern, M.F. & Hoeltzel, R. (2002). *Responsible Drinking: A Moderation Management Approach for Problem Drinkers.* Berkeley: New Harbinger.

Rotgers, F. & Davis, B. A. (2006). *Treating Alcohol Problems.* New York: John Wiley.

Andrew Tatarsky
Tatarsky, A. (2002). *Harm Reduction Psychotherapy: A New Treatment for Drug and Alcohol Problems.* Northvale, N.J.: Jason Aronson.

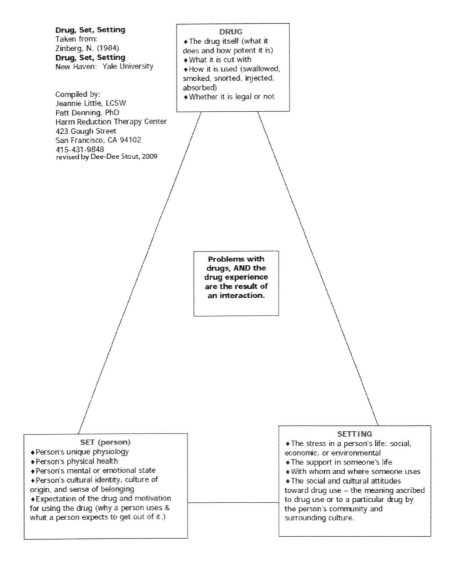

The Twelve Steps of Alcoholics Anonymous

1. We admitted we were powerless over alcohol—that our lives had become unmanageable.

2. Came to believe that a Power greater than ourselves could restore us to sanity.

3. Made a decision to turn our will and our lives over to the care of God as we understood Him.

4. Made a searching and fearless moral inventory of ourselves.

5. Admitted to God, to ourselves, and to another human being the exact nature of our wrongs.

6. Were entirely ready to have God remove all these defects of character.

7. Humbly asked Him to remove our shortcomings.

8. Made a list of all persons we had harmed and became willing to make amends to them all.

9. Made direct amends to such people wherever possible, except when to do so would injure them or others.

10. Continued to take personal inventory and when we were wrong promptly admitted it.

11. Sought through prayer and meditation to improve our conscious contact with God, as we understood Him, praying only for knowledge of His will for us and the power to carry that out.

12. Having had a spiritual awakening as the result of these Steps, we tried to carry this message to alcoholics, and to practice these principles in all our affairs.

Copyright © A.A. World Services, Inc.
www.aa.org

The New Professional's 12- Steps[63]

Step 1: Admitted that we were powerless over our clients and their behavior changes, and that our profession had become unmanageable.

Step 2: Came to believe that a power greater than us - our clients' will and determination - could restore our profession to sanity.

Step 3: Made a decision to turn our will over to our clients, to let them run their own lives, as they seek a better understanding of their values and preferences.

Step 4: Made a searching and fearless moral inventory of our professional selves and our profession.

Step 5: Admitted to ourselves, and our clients, the exact nature of our wrongs.

Step 6: Were entirely ready to have these wrongs removed from our profession.

Step 7: Humbly asked how to remove these wrongs from our profession (which may mean removing some clinicians), and sought guidance from all sources on ideas of how to do so.

Step 8: Made a list of all persons we had harmed professionally and became willing to make amends to them all – including us and the profession.

Step 9: Made direct amends to clients and others, wherever possible, except when to do so would injure them.

Step 10: Continued to take professional inventory and when we were wrong, promptly admitted it - and took Steps to see it wouldn't occur again.

Step 11: Sought through meditation (*listening*) to improve our conscious contact with clients, asking only for the will & power to carry out our creed, "First, do no harm," and guide clients to discover their own goals & recover their own lives.

Step 12: Having had an "A-Ha!" moment as the result of these Steps, we agreed to carry the message of 12-Stepping-Harm Reduction - and all other client-centered methodologies - to others within our profession and out, and to practice these principles in all our profession's affairs.

Harm Reduction Mnemonic
(with thanks to Sharon Harger)

Harm Reduction is...

Helping
Advocating
Reducing recidivism
Mending wounds

Reinforcing healthier options
Educating
Delivering hope
Uncovering challenges
Celebrating choice
Treatment opportunities
Investing your time
Offering support &
Never, ever giving up on your client!

ENDNOTES

1 Author's Note: It was suggested that I might be breaking with the 10th Tradition of AA by disclosing my full name and talking about 12-Step/AA. To those who would say this, I say I understand. I simply didn't know of any other way to write this book that would have meaning. If I did NOT disclose, I could be discounted as not understanding 12-Step and AA; and if I did, I would potentially be breaking tradition. I am sorry if this upsets or disappoints anyone, and I would hope that 12-Steppers would remember two things: Bill Wilson disclosed his membership in AA constantly, and I was taught that, on occasion, we may break anonymity as long as we aren't speaking for all of AA or its members, but only for ourselves. Many others seemed to agree and agreed to the use of their names here for the purpose of having an open dialogue. I hope you will respect their decision, and mine.
2 See Hubble, M., Miller, S., & Duncan, B. *The Heart and Soul of Change: What Works in Therapy.* (1999) APA.
3 See Miller, W.R., & Rollnick, S. *Motivational Interviewing: Preparing People for Change,* 2nd Edition. (2002) The Guilford Press. NY, NY.
4 White, W.L. *Slaying the Dragon: The History of Addiction Treatment and Recovery in the America.* (1998) Chestnut Health Systems. Chicago, IL.
5 *Alcoholics Anonymous*, 3rd Edition (1976). AAWS.
6 Narcotics Anonymous, 6th Edition (2008), NAWS, Chatsworth, CA. p3.
7 Denning, P. *Practicing Harm Reduction Psychotherapy.* (2002) The Guilford Press.
8 See "The Continuum of Alcohol and other Drug Use" chart by Jeannie Little, Director, Harm Reduction Therapy Center, in the Appendix.
9 From Alcoholics Anonymous, 4th Edition, (2008) AAWS. Online version. p. 60.
10 Marlatt, G.A. & Gordon, J.M. *Relapse Prevention.* (1985). The Guilford Press.
11 Gorski, T. & Miller, M. *Mistaken Beliefs.* (1988) Herald House Publishing.
12 Mark Thornton, O. P. Alford III Assistant Professor of Economics at Auburn University. *Policy Analysis no.157,* July 17, 1991.The CATO Institute. www.cato.org/pub_display.php?pub_id=1017.
13 Wikipedia. Prohibition in the United States. 2.29.08
14 The 21st Amendment passed in Feb. 20, 1933.
15 Dr. William Silkworth was the medical director of Charles B. Towns Hospital in New York where he treated some fifty thousand alcoholics in his lifetime. He was an important friend to AA and Bill Wilson, and wrote the chapter in *Alcoholics Anonymous*, "The Doctor's Opinion." Kurtz, E.

Not-God, Hazelden, 1991. p23.
16 Aaron, Paul, and Musto, David. Temperance and Prohibition in America: An Historical Overview. In: Moore, Mark H., and Gerstein, Dean R. (eds.) Alcohol and Public Policy: Beyond the Shadow of Prohibition. Washington, DC: National Academy Press, 1981. pp. 127-181.
17 Listen to the speech here: www.aa.org/en_gso_archives.cfm?PageID=22&SubPage=150
18 Twelve Steps and Twelve Traditions. Alcoholics Anonymous World Services, Inc: NY, NY. 1981. pg106.
19 Kurtz, E. *Not-God*. p21.
20 This is AA: An Introduction to the AA Recovery Program (pamphlet). AA World Services, Inc. (AAWS), 1984.
21 *Alcoholics Anonymous*, 3rd Edition; p.31.
22 Ibid. p. 85.
23 Author's note: Bill Wilson originally wanted the Preamble in *Alcoholics Anonymous* to read, "The only requirement for membership is a *sincere* desire to stop drinking." [Emphasis mine] Dr. Bob cautioned against this qualifier, asking him who would be in charge of determining who was "serious" and who was not? The word was dropped.
24 "Actually, some groups did; that is why AA dropped the word "honest" from the membership requirement." Personal communication, Ernie Kurtz (2008).
25 Alcoholics Anonymous, 3rd Edition. p38-9.
26 *A Reference Guide to the Big Book of Alcoholics Anonymous*. By Stewart C., (1986) Seattle, WA. Recovery Press. p118; 120-23.
27 *Alcoholics Anonymous*, 3rd Edition. p164.
28 *Alcoholics Anonymous*, 3rd Edition. p95.
29 *Alcoholics Anonymous*, 3rd Edition. p100-1.
30 Personal communication.
31 As AA's 4th Tradition states in the *Twelve Steps and Twelve Traditions* (1981, p146): "Each group should be autonomous except in matters affecting other groups or A.A. as a whole." This is because each group can decide for themselves how they will conduct a meeting within basic General Service Office guidelines for continuity.
32 *Open* meetings may be attended by anyone interested in AA. *Closed* refers to those meetings reserved for those with alcohol problems only. See www.aa.org for more.
33 Tradition 11: *Our public relations policy is based on attraction rather than promotion; we need always maintain personal anonymity at the level of press, radio and films.*
34 Tradition 4: *Each group should be autonomous except in matters affecting AA as a whole.*
35 Tradition 10: *Alcoholics Anonymous has no opinion on outside issues; hence the A.A. name ought never be drawn into public controversy.*
36 *"Service meetings"* are meetings of those elected members of AA

who hold "office," such as the secretary of the meeting or the General Service Representative, to relay information about the desires of the AA members of a geographical area to Central Office in New York. As AA's governance is an upside-down triangle- the members are on top and in charge -and the authority of Central Office – at the bottom of the triangle - simply implements the will of its members. See www.aa.org for more information on this unique governing system. See www.AA.org for more.

37 In the United States, courts have ruled since 1996 that inmates, parolees and probationers cannot be ordered to attend a religious based program such as AA or other recovery programs that have substantial religious components since such coercion is in violation of the Establishment Clause of the First Amendment of the Constitution. Wikipedia, *Alcoholics Anonymous: Court Rulings*. 3.4.08.

38 *Twelve Steps and Twelve Traditions*, p166.

39 Wikipedia. *Bill W., The Final Years*. 3.4.08.

40 *AA Fact File*, p11.

41 While the disease concept was nothing new to AA, AA had held no general opinion of the actual scientific facts of such a concept, preferring to defer to their 10th Tradition on outside issues. Bill W. did not use the term "disease," preferring instead the term "illness" or "condition" or "spiritual malady" to describe alcoholism. Today's AA appears to endorse using the term "disease." (This is important enough to be in the text as an explanation of how the disease model became popular in AA –along with a discussion of the repercussions.

42 It is interesting to note the distrust shared by many members of AA regarding psychology due to the close friendship and important contributions of Carl Jung to both Bill Wilson and AA.

43 In the 1990's GSO distributed a card that individual meetings could decide to read at the start of a meeting re: AA's singleness of purpose, asking that members hold their conversations to alcohol only.

44 NA; the second largest 12-Step fellowship in the US devoted to assisting users of drugs other than alcohol. See www.NA.org for more.

45 *Alcoholics Anonymous*, 3rd Edition. p550.

46 Ibid.

47 Exact quotation: "Neither the efforts of dedicated clinicians nor the individual's own willpower appear to be able to cure an alcoholic's conditioned habit at a given time. Our task is to provide emergency medical care, shelter, detoxification, and understanding until self-healing takes place." George Vaillant, *The Natural History of Alcoholism*, 1983, p314-5.

48 Audrey Kishline is the founder of Moderation Management. To read her letter to MM regarding her decision to abstain from alcohol prior to the accident, see www.doctordeluca.com/Documents/KishlineToldMM.htm.

49 Miller, W.R. & Munoz, R. *Controlling your Drinking: Tools to Make Moderation Work for You.* (2004) The Guilford Press.
50 Biernacki, Patrick. *Pathways from Heroin Addiction: Recovery Without Treatment* (Health, Society, and Policy). 1986. No publisher found.
51 *The Diagnostic and Statistical Manual of Mental Disorders, DSM IV-TR (2000)*, published by the American Psychological Association.
52 Miller, W.R. & Rollnick, S. (1992) *Motivational Interviewing: Preparing People to Change Addictive Behavior.* The Guilford Press.
53 Miller, W.R. & Munoz, R. (1975) *Controlling Your Drinking: Tools to Make Moderation Work for You.* (2004) The Guilford Press.
54 See the seminal work, *Moderation as a Goal or Outcome of Treatment for Alcohol Problems* (1987), Haworth Press, by Linda and Mark Sobell, for more on this.
55 Marsh, E. *Physician, Heal Thyself: 35 Years of Adventures in Sobriety by an AA Oldtimer* (1988). Compcare Publications. Dr. Marsh was also the author of the chapter of the same name in *Alcoholics Anonymous* as well as a good friend of Bill Wilson's, who was also Dr. Marsh's AA sponsor before his death.
56 In a personal communication in 1995 with Lisa Najavits, Harvard researcher and author of *Seeking Safety*, she suggested that trauma should not be discussed in early recovery generally as it is too often re-traumatizing to the individual.
57 This was said often by my former boss, the Program Director, Rich Pelletier, now long deceased.
58 Miller, W.R. & Rollnick, S. *Motivational Interviewing: Preparing People to Change Addictive Behavior* (1992). The Guilford Press.
59 Denning, P., Little, J., and Glick, A. *Over the Influence: The Harm Reduction Guide to Managing Drugs and Alcohol.* (2004) The Guilford Press.
60 Denning, P. *Practicing Harm Reduction Psychotherapy: An Alternative Approach to Addictions*, The Guilford Press (2004).
61 "Having had a spiritual awakening as the result of these steps, we tried to carry this message to alcoholics, and to practice these principles in all our affairs." *Alcoholics Anonymous*, 3rd Edition, p60.
62 It has been stated that 60% of US businesses maintain a zero tolerance policy to addictions therefore no treatment will be offered when a worker is caught using drugs, including alcohol. Only in those cases where a union is involved is that policy different, based on their ability to negotiate other outcomes.
63 Based on the original 12 Steps found in AA's "*Twelve Steps and Twelve Traditions*," (AA World Services, Inc).

INDEX

A

abstinence ix, xiv, xvii, xix, xxi, xxii, xxiii, xxv, 3, 4, 5, 7, 8, 16, 21, 37, 44, 45, 46, 47, 48, 50, 56, 57, 59, 67, 69, 71, 79, 80, 81, 83, 84, 85, 88, 91, 108, 110, 112, 117, 118, 119, 122, 127, 128, 130, 133, 134, 142, 144, 146, 149, 150, 154, 155, 156, 157
Abstinence Movement 13
Abuse and Addiction (NIAAA) 56
abuse cycle 35
active users xi, 101, 102, 129
acute intoxication 148
addiction i, ix, x, xiv, xv, xviii, xxiii, xxiv, xxv, 1, 2, 3, 12, 23, 24, 25, 26, 28, 33, 39, 40, 41, 42, 43, 44, 45, 46, 47, 49, 51, 55, 58, 59, 60, 75, 76, 77, 78, 79, 80, 82, 86, 87, 88, 90, 102, 119, 120, 121, 126, 127, 131, 132, 133, 134, 139, 156, 157, 158
Addiction Treatment i, ix, x, xviii, xxiv, 12, 23, 25, 26, 28, 39, 40, 46, 49, 51, 80, 86, 87, 88, 90, 139
addictive 35, 40, 41, 76, 77, 90, 160
addicts x, 2, 34, 41, 108, 111, 119, 120, 132, 134, 136, 154, 157
AIDS 23, 24, 25, 26, 34, 92, 95, 96, 116
alcohol i, ix, xviii, xxi, xxv, 8, 12, 13, 14, 15, 16, 18, 20, 21, 24, 25, 26, 31, 33, 37, 44, 48, 54, 56, 57, 58, 60, 61, 62, 64, 68, 72, 78, 80, 81, 82, 84, 85, 87, 88, 93, 94, 98, 99, 100, 103, 115, 117, 118, 122, 134, 135, 136, 139, 141, 143, 147, 148, 149, 151, 153, 156, 160, 161, 163, 166, 167, 168, 169
alcohol dependence 56, 58, 62, 78
Alcoholics Anonymous (AA) xviii, 137
alcoholism xv, 15, 18, 21, 24, 28, 39, 62, 81, 159, 160, 168
Allan Clear 95, 98, 159
Alternatives (ATA) 36
amphetamines 123
Andrew Tatarsky 60, 84, 85, 87, 94, 159, 161
Annie Fahy 99, 104
anti-addictive mechanisms 77
anxiety 45, 64
aversion therapy 58, 63, 64

B

behavior x, xxiii, xxiv, 4, 5, 6, 7, 8, 9, 28, 40, 41, 43, 47, 50, 54, 57, 58, 59, 60, 63, 64, 65, 71, 92, 104, 140, 157, 158, 160, 164
behavioral counseling 63, 64
behavioral therapy 37, 57, 58
Betty Ford Clinics 44
Bill Wilson xiv, xv, xxi, xxii, xxv, 12, 14, 15, 18, 21, 22, 103, 166, 167, 168, 169
biological 58, 59
biopsychosocial 58, 59, 94
bipolar disorder 144

C

causal factors 58
chaotic users 108
chemicals 33
Chicago Recovery Alliance 10, 27, 29, 137, 159
Chuck Ries 122, 130, 159
cigarettes 76, 135
class 16, 30, 34, 39, 71, 78, 113, 125, 132
clean 70, 74, 105, 106, 107, 115, 116, 118, 126, 127, 128, 136, 144, 145
client i, xxiii, xxiv, 4, 6, 8, 32, 37, 40, 43, 44, 47, 48, 54, 55, 89, 90, 91, 92, 102, 103, 104, 109, 110, 111, 112, 113, 114, 117, 118, 133, 138, 141, 146, 164, 165
client-centered 146, 164
clinic 32, 33, 35, 36, 81, 87, 88, 89, 117, 127
clinicians xxiii, 32, 37, 60, 63, 142, 164, 168
cocaine 14, 77, 100, 123
cognitive-behavioral therapy 37
cognitive dissonance 46
compassion ii, 26, 116, 138, 146
compulsive 12, 127
confrontation 34, 51
consequences x, 40, 59, 82, 122
continuum 4, 59, 60, 133, 155, 157
controlled drinking 16, 56, 57, 63, 65, 66, 148
coping 61, 107
coping mechanism 107
counseling 26, 63, 64, 87, 99, 100, 102, 103, 110, 113, 139, 140, 141, 153
counselors xxi, 82, 85, 94
countertransference 37, 54, 90
crack 69, 108, 111
criminal justice xiii, xiv, 7, 71, 132
cutting 79, 103

D

Dan Bigg 10, 23, 29, 137, 159
Dee-Dee Stout i, ii, ix, x, xx, 137, 146, 159
denial 7, 9, 49, 154
dependence 9, 56, 58, 62, 78, 83, 157, 160
depression 45, 60, 64, 140, 144
destructive 73, 106, 125
detox 44, 102, 119, 150
diagnosis 35, 36, 37, 49, 51, 60, 62
dialogue 92, 166
dirty 70, 88, 116
disease model 12, 58, 59, 88, 168
doctors 27, 32, 99
domestic violence 13, 49, 101
dope 104, 108, 123, 124, 125, 126, 133
Dr. Bob xv, xxv, 12, 15, 16, 20, 21, 22, 167
drug i, ii, x, xi, xiii, xv, xvi, xxi, xxii, xxv, 4, 5, 6, 7, 8, 9, 10, 12, 20, 21, 24, 25, 26, 27, 28, 30, 31, 33, 34, 37, 39, 54, 57, 61, 70, 71, 72, 73, 74, 76, 77, 78, 79, 80, 81, 82, 85, 87, 88, 89, 91, 92, 93, 94, 95, 96, 97, 98, 104, 105, 106, 107, 108, 113, 115, 116, 120, 121, 122, 123, 124, 125, 127, 128, 129, 130, 131, 132, 133, 134, 135, 136, 139, 141, 144, 145, 153, 156, 157, 160
drug-free 26, 144
drug laws 82, 121
Drug Policy Alliance 37
drug tests 7
drug users ii, x, xiii, 5, 10, 20, 21, 26, 39, 70, 73, 74, 81, 92, 93, 96, 98, 108, 127, 128
Drug War 72, 131
drunk ix, 7, 16, 18, 33, 48, 61,

100, 148, 151
DSM 9, 78, 83, 169
dual diagnosis 37, 49, 51
DUI x, 83, 113
dysfunctional 72, 73

E

Edward Reed 119, 159
electrical aversion therapy 58, 63, 64
empathy xxiv, 26, 65, 116
empowerment 43, 91
enabling 97
enforcement 121, 124
environment 53, 108, 110, 118, 123
evidence-based 37, 85, 160

F

factors 58, 59, 108
fear 27, 41
Fibromyalgia Syndrome (FMS) 143
Fred Rotgers 80, 86, 161
functional alcoholic 148

G

G. Alan Marlatt xi, 56, 61, 159, 160
gender-specific treatment 100
genetics 108, 123
gradualists 55
group homes 49

H

habit 105, 168
Harm Reduction xiii, xvi, 1, 3, 4, 12, 23, 30, 32, 35, 36, 38, 39, 44, 49, 55, 56, 62, 69, 75, 80, 82, 84, 87, 98, 104, 125, 142, 143, 159, 161, 164, 165, 166, 169
Harm Reduction Coalition 32, 35, 98, 143, 159

harm reduction psychotherapy 36, 37, 38, 48, 91, 94, 160
health i, xiii, xv, xxiii, xxiv, xxv, 3, 5, 9, 10, 12, 26, 32, 33, 35, 36, 37, 39, 40, 45, 49, 71, 81, 83, 91, 92, 94, 97, 100, 101, 102, 109, 117, 120, 121, 124, 127, 137, 139, 143, 149, 155, 156, 158, 160
health insurance 124
helplessness model 59
heroin 6, 10, 27, 41, 42, 53, 73, 76, 79, 108, 116, 117, 119, 120, 121, 123, 126, 141, 144, 169
high-functioning 47
high-risk 57, 58, 77, 129, 148
hitting bottom 16, 59
HIV 23, 24, 25, 26, 27, 28, 32, 34, 35, 57, 72, 92, 95, 106, 108, 116, 126, 127, 154, 155
HIVIES 23, 24, 27
homeless x, 42, 49, 51, 53, 107, 127, 153

I

illegal xiv, 31
Imani Woods 153, 155
incarceration 25, 92
injection drug use 57, 124
inoculation 67
inpatient 20, 26, 49, 59, 62
integrative 55, 87, 91
integrative harm reduction 91
integrative psychoanalytical 87
internalized oppression 70
intervention 52, 57, 64, 82, 128, 155, 156
intoxicant 43, 122
intoxication 42, 148
intuition 92

J

jail 7, 8, 73, 82, 108, 124, 133
Jeannie Little xxiii, 37, 49, 55, 102, 118, 142, 159, 160, 166
junkie 151

L

Larry Walton 147, 152
laypersons 37
legal xiv, xv, 81, 121, 135
leverage 7, 44
Lisa Moore 69, 74
loaded 142
Lochlan McHale 109, 114

M

maladaptive behavior 43
Marc Kern 44, 159, 161
Mark Kinzly 105, 108
meditation 60, 61, 163, 164
mental health 9, 26, 32, 33, 35, 36, 37, 39, 40, 45, 49, 83, 94, 97, 100, 101, 149, 160
methadone xxi, xxv, 25, 60, 108, 115, 116, 117, 118, 119, 120, 121, 126, 131, 132, 134, 135, 137
methamphetamine 5, 53
methamphetamine psychosis 5
mindfulness 60, 145
Minnesota Recovery Alliance 23
moderation 37, 44, 46, 48, 59, 65, 66, 67, 82, 83, 84, 85, 161, 168, 169
Moderation Management 44, 83, 84, 161, 168
mood 64
moral inventory 139, 163, 164
morbidity 121
mortality 121
motivation 7, 23, 127
motivational interviewing xxiii, 7, 26, 37, 40, 64, 65, 68, 83, 85, 100, 104, 110, 113, 134, 136, 137, 140, 141, 142, 146, 156, 158, 159, 166, 169
multi-modality 87

N

narcotics 21, 115, 135, 150, 155, 166
Narcotics Anonymous (NA) 135
National Institute of Alcohol 56
needle exchange xviii, 29, 32, 35, 60, 79, 81, 82, 85, 89, 96, 106, 127, 138
negotiation 92
neurochemical 143
newcomers 150
non-judgmental 52, 90, 156
nurses 32, 49, 99

O

old timers 150
opiate 116, 119
outpatient 20, 26, 32, 34, 88, 100
outreach 32, 96, 149
overdosing 93

P

(PDR) 30, 33
pain xxii, 35, 79, 99, 103, 121, 143, 144
Pam Smithstan 131, 136
paradigm i, xiii, xxiv, 12, 46, 47, 55, 88, 89, 91, 157
Patt Denning xvi, xix, xxiii, 3, 30, 38, 60, 76, 102, 143, 144, 159, 160
pharmacology 33, 36
physician 12, 33, 41, 143
Physician's Desk Reference 30
police 27, 81, 82, 107
politics 83, 84
positive change xxii, xxiii, xxv, 10,

28, 29
powerlessness ix, 43, 59
prescriptions 30
prevalence 77
prevention xix, xxiii, 23, 27, 35, 57, 58, 63, 80, 138, 160
prison 13, 66, 80, 84, 116, 117
private practice 36, 40, 48, 88, 94, 140
programmed relapses 80, 81
prohibition xiii, 13, 14, 166, 167
prostitution 133
psychiatrist 48, 60, 61, 66, 124, 145
psychoactive substances 41
psychodynamic construct 37
psychologist 36, 40, 45, 62, 68, 80, 87
psychology 26, 45, 60, 76, 160, 168
psychotherapy 8, 36, 37, 38, 48, 60, 89, 91, 93, 94, 160
PTSD 51
public health xiii, 12, 32, 37, 57, 71, 102, 142, 155, 160

Q

Quaaludes 44, 45

R

race xiv, 15, 71
rationalization 154
re-acculturate 52
recovery i, xi, xiii, xiv, xxi, xxii, xxiv, xxv, 1, 2, 3, 5, 10, 13, 15, 18, 22, 23, 24, 26, 28, 39, 47, 60, 71, 74, 85, 96, 97, 98, 100, 104, 115, 116, 119, 122, 123, 127, 134, 135, 136, 138, 139, 140, 142, 144, 145, 146, 149, 150, 151, 152, 155, 160, 161, 168, 169
rehabilitation 119

relapse xix, xxiii, 4, 57, 58, 61, 67, 80, 84, 116, 138, 145, 157, 160
relapse management 57
relapse prevention xix, xxiii, 57, 58, 80, 138, 160
religion 42
religious model 39
repression 25
residential treatment xxii, 6, 49, 139, 140, 141
resistance xxiv, 35, 37, 113, 158
risk 25, 57, 58, 59, 63, 77, 78, 91, 92, 98, 104, 113, 124, 129, 148, 160

S

schizophrenia 31
secondary prevention 57, 63
Secular Organization for 46
self-disclosure 153
self-efficacy xxiv, 78
self-empowerment 43
self-help 13, 64, 65, 94
self-medicate 60, 79
self-monitoring 63
sex 23, 25, 30, 31, 41, 42, 95, 107, 109, 126
side effects 121
sleep problems 64
smoking 111, 134, 135
sober 16, 61, 70, 84, 107, 110, 115, 116, 118, 122, 128, 135, 136, 138, 144, 145, 150, 153, 155
sobriety xxiv, xxv, 15, 20, 21, 69, 70, 80, 88, 96, 142, 145, 149, 156
Sobriety (SOS) 46, 169
social justice 128
social services 49
social support 70, 73
social worker 93, 133, 153
speed x, 123

stabilization 51, 120
Stages of Change Theory 140
Stanton Peele 40, 62, 75, 79, 159, 161
Steve M. 115
stigma 100
stigmatization 25, 71, 92, 93
stimulants 123
stress 32, 33, 51, 124, 140, 143
stress users 33
substance abuse i, xiv, 32, 33, 35, 36, 49, 51, 83, 90, 92, 149, 153, 154, 160
substance abusers 33, 77
substitution 26
support x, xix, xxiv, 1, 7, 8, 16, 19, 23, 27, 28, 35, 70, 73, 83, 96, 102, 117, 122, 125, 151, 156, 165
symptomology 45
symptoms 9, 17, 45, 58, 148

T

12-Step i, ii, ix, xiv, xv, xvii, xviii, xix, xxiii, 2, 3, 8, 10, 12, 16, 19, 23, 24, 39, 40, 42, 43, 45, 47, 53, 55, 68, 76, 85, 88, 94, 97, 102, 103, 105, 107, 108, 110, 112, 115, 117, 118, 128, 132, 135, 136, 138, 139, 142, 144, 149, 150, 151, 152, 154, 156, 157, 158, 161, 166, 168
Temperance Movement 13
The Big Book xxii, 16, 34, 35, 167
theory xxii, xxiv, 3, 4, 6, 40, 53, 92, 140
therapeutic community 80, 94
therapist 33, 35, 54, 64, 65, 90, 91, 92, 160
therapy x, 17, 20, 35, 37, 39, 43, 46, 47, 49, 57, 58, 61, 63, 64, 65, 88, 89, 91, 97, 104, 151, 160
Tom Horvath 39
traditional treatment ix, xxv, 7, 27, 83, 85, 102, 111
transference 37
Transtheoretical Model 140
trauma 37, 54, 101, 143, 146, 169
treatment i, ix, x, xi, xiii, xiv, xv, xviii, xxi, xxii, xxiii, xxiv, xxv, 2, 3, 4, 5, 6, 7, 8, 9, 10, 12, 19, 20, 21, 23, 24, 25, 26, 27, 28, 29, 32, 33, 34, 35, 36, 37, 38, 39, 40, 43, 44, 46, 47, 48, 49, 50, 51, 53, 54, 55, 56, 57, 58, 60, 61, 63, 64, 65, 67, 70, 71, 73, 74, 79, 80, 81, 82, 83, 84, 85, 86, 87, 88, 89, 90, 93, 94, 99, 100, 101, 102, 105, 106, 107, 108, 111, 119, 120, 123, 127, 128, 129, 130, 134, 135, 136, 139, 140, 141, 143, 145, 149, 150, 151, 153, 154, 155, 156, 157, 158, 160, 169
triggered 8
triggers 63
tweaking 53

V

Valium 45

W

War on Drugs x, xiii, 131, 134
William Miller xxiv, 37, 140

X

Xanax 45

Z

zero tolerance xiv, 156, 157, 169

Printed in Great Britain
by Amazon